A REVIVED
MODERN
CLASSIC

THREE ITALIAN CHRONICLES

ALSO BY STENDHAL
AVAILABLE FROM NEW DIRECTIONS

The Pink & The Green
Translated by Richard Howard

The Telegraph
Translated by Louise Varèse

STENDHAL
THREE ITALIAN CHRONICLES

TRANSLATED BY C. K. SCOTT-MONCRIEFF

INTRODUCTION BY RICHARD HOWARD

A NEW DIRECTIONS PAPERBOOK

The contents of this selection are taken from *The Shorter
Novels of Stendhal* (Liveright, 1946).

Manufactured in the United States of America.
New Directions Books are printed on acid-free paper.
First published as New Directions Paperbook 704 in 1991
as part of the *Revived Modern Classics Series*.

Library of Congress Cataloging-in-Publication Data

Stendhal, 1783-1842.
    [Selections. English. 1991]
    Three Italian chronicles / Stendhal ; translated by
    C. K. Scott
-Moncrieff ; with an introduction by Richard Howard.
        p.   cm. — (A New Directions paperback ; 704)
(A Revived modern classic)
    Translated from French.
    Contents: The cenci — The abbess of Castro — Vanina
    Vanini.
    ISBN 0-8112-1150-9 (alk. paper)
    1. Stendhal, 1783-1842—Translations, English.
    2. Italy—Fiction.
I. Title.   II. Series.
PQ2435.A3S37   1991
843'.7—dc20   90-35325
                                               CIP

New Directions Books are published for James Laughlin
by New Directions Publishing Corporation,
80 Eighth Avenue, New York 10011

CONTENTS

BEYLE'S TALES

by Richard Howard

Vanina Vanini was published in 1829, signed "Stendhal" (a pen name of Marie Henri Beyle), a year before *The Red and the Black*. It is the only one of the eight "Italian chronicles" set in the nineteenth century, and apparently the author desired to show that contemporary Italians could be identified with those of the sixteenth when, as Beyle says, "a man could distinguish himself by *all forms* of merit." The great Beylist M. Martineau regards the tale as a sort of homage to the friends of Métilde Visconti and to the passion for liberty cherished by that ideal beloved. A four-act play based on the piece was published in Berlin in 1896, and a film version produced quite recently; Beyle himself, eleven years after the tale was published, wrote to Balzac that he had made "plans for a novel, for example *Vanina,* but making a plan turns me off; I dictate 25 or 30 pages, then evening comes and I need some strong *distraction;* I have to have forgotten everything the next morning; by reading the last three or four pages of the chapter written the day before, the next day's chapter comes to me." But ultimately it failed to come, and the stark, staring little *conte,* with its betraying heroine who is herself betrayed by her own passion (rather like Mina de Vanghel, whose story was written the next year as well), stands as the first of what Beyle was to call his *Chroniques italiennes* (published as such, posthumously, in 1855).

All the others, of which the two given here are the finest, are "based on," "drawn from," "variations of" a group of old Italian narratives, popular romances and sensational cases which Beyle either purchased or had copied from manuscripts in various libraries. *The Cenci* appeared unsigned in the *Revue des Deux Mondes* in 1837, when Guido Reni's painting of the Samian Sibyl—which Beyle had seen and greatly admired in the Palazzo Barberini—still passed for the authentic portrait of Beatrice Cenci. Beyle was also familiar with Shelley's tragedy (1819) and with the Marquis de Custine's (1830), and found the gruesome legend of parricide and punishment alluring. In 1833 he had written in the margins of an edition of his own *Promenades dans Rome:* "Beatrice Cenci—nothing more difficult than to get at the truth. A lot of pseudo-novels, as in Vallardi's almanac *Non ti scordar di che.* . . . Farinacci's 11 volumes the best source." And in 1839, in two numbers of the same review, signed F. de Lagenevais, appeared *The Abbess of Castro,* the last of Beyle's tales to be published in periodical form; with *The Cenci,* this piece appeared as a book a few months later, the same year as *The Charterhouse of Parma* (written in fifty-two days!). In 1840, a five-act play more or less inspired by Beyle's (unacknowledged) text was performed for a month in Paris, but the grim novella seems to have had no further echo. It is interesting, however, that Beyle noted on his copy of the Italian manuscript of 1572: "first *historiette* bought in Mantua, this is the first to be transcribed by me, it has encouraged me to brave the wretched dust of libraries."

Unsigned or pseudonymous (I suppose no author but Kierkegaard has ever had a more vexed relation to authenticity), these tales must bear a special relation to the writer's *proper person:* Beyle wanted to revoke his filial status (he signs his letters to his sister Pauline "the bastard"), and to give himself not only a new countenance, one that would have nothing to do with the despised Chérubin Beyle, but a new destiny, a new social standing, even a new *fatherland* (Stendhal is the name of a Prussian town). It will not surprise us that as the last Cosmopolite (eighteenth century) and the first Good European (nineteenth century), the creator of these Italian chronicles should adopt multiple nationalities—German, English, Italian, anything but French. Beyle had over a hundred pseudonyms—as Jean Starobinski, in his brilliant study "Stendhal pseudonyme," observes, it is the demon who says My name is Legion.

Whether Beyle actually believed these narratives were the original and contemporary sources of the events recounted is anything but certain; it is likely that he regarded himself as yet one more modulator in the sequence of *tellings,* a *raconteur* with his own program and, to use a word he would have enjoyed, agenda. What he reported about his "originals" (and his "translations" of them) was intended to tempt publishers, to seduce editors of reviews, and to attract readers. For himself, he recognized in such "documents" his secret desires, those elements of cruelty and energy in passion which might give life all its savor, all its worth. Lucidity and exactitude were part of the appeal as well—his dislike of exaggeration is suggested by a note scribbled in 1834: "A young woman murdered right next to me—I run to the spot, she is lying in the middle of the street and beside her head a puddle of blood about a foot across. This is what M. Victor Hugo calls being bathed in one's own blood."

And of course such things happen—and have always happened—in Italy, that Italy which he says is "in truth merely an occasion for sensations." Of course by sensations he means, I think, a more intense life, a finer, richer energy of consciousness, something that Robert Browning too must have meant when he found his Old Yellow Book in the second-hand market in Florence:

> Here it is, this I toss and take again;
> Small-quarto size, part print part manuscript:
> A book in shape but really pure crude fact
> Secreted from man's life when hearts beat hard,
> And brains, high-blooded, ticked two centuries since.
> Give it me back! The thing's restorative
> I' the touch and sight.

For Beyle too, Italy *ab illo tempore* was when men were not—as they are in France—pusillanimous, when they did not—as they do in France—heed the voice of prejudice, when they had—as they haven't in France—no fear of ridicule, and when above all they could—as they cannot in France—speak and act upon the hearts and bodies of women.

THE CENCI

THE CENCI

1599

THE Don Juan of Molière is, unquestionably, a rake,
but first and foremost he is a man of the world;
before giving way to the irresistible inclination that
attracts him to pretty women, he feels that he must con-
form to a certain ideal standard, he seeks to be the type
of man that would be most admired at the court of a young
king of gallantry and parts.

The Don Juan of Mozart is already more true to nature,
and less French, he thinks less of *what other people will
say;* his first care is not for appearances, is not *parestre,* to
quote d'Aubigné's *Baron de Fœneste.* We have but two
portraits of the Italian Don Juan, as he must have ap-
peared, in that fair land, in the sixteenth century, in the
dawn of the new civilisation.

Of these two portraits, there is one which I simply cannot
display, our generation is too straitlaced; one has to re-
mind oneself of that great expression which I used often
to hear Lord Byron repeat: "This age of cant." This
tiresome form of hypocrisy, which takes in no one, has the
great advantage of giving fools something to say: they
express their horror that people have ventured to mention
this, or to laugh at that, etc. Its disadvantage is that it
vastly restricts the field of history.

If the reader has the good taste to allow me, I intend
to offer him, in all humility, an historical notice of the
second of these Don Juans, of whom it is possible to speak
in 1837; his name was Francesco Cenci.

To render a Don Juan possible, there must be hypocrisy

[3]

in society. A Don Juan would have been an effect without a cause in the ancient world; religion was a matter for rejoicing, it urged men to take their pleasure; how could it have punished people who make a certain pleasure their whole business in life? The government alone spoke of *abstinence,* it forbade things that might harm the state, that is to say the common interest of all, and not what might harm the individual actor.

And so any man with a taste for women and plenty of money could be a Don Juan in Athens; no one would have made any objection; no one professed that this life is a vale of tears and that there is merit in inflicting suffering on oneself.

I do not think that the Athenian Don Juan could arrive at the criminal stage as rapidly as the Don Juan of a modern monarchy; a great part of the latter's pleasure consists in challenging public opinion, and he has made a start, in his youth, by imagining that he was only challenging hypocrisy.

To break the laws under a monarchy like that of Louis XV, to fire a shot at a slater and bring him crashing down from his roof, does not that prove that one moves in royal circles, has the best possible tone, and laughs at one's judge, who is a *bourgeois? To laugh at the judge,* is not that the first exploit of every little incipient Don Juan?

With us, women are no longer in fashion, that is why the Don Juan type is rare; but when it existed, such men invariably began by seeking quite natural pleasures, boasting the while of their courage in challenging ideas which seemed to them not to be founded on reason in the religion of their contemporaries. It is only later on, and when he is beginning to become perverted that your Don Juan finds an exquisite pleasure in challenging opinions which he himself feels to be just and rational.

This transition must have been difficult and rare in an-

cient times, and it is only when we come to the Roman
Emperors, after Tiberius and Capri, that we find libertines
who love corruption for its own sake, that is to say for
the pleasure of challenging the rational opinions of their
contemporaries.

Thus it is to the Christian religion that I ascribe the
possibility of the Satanic part played by Don Juan. It
was this religion, doubtless, which taught the world that
a poor slave, a gladiator had a soul absolutely equal in
capacity to that of Cæsar himself; we have, therefore, to
thank it for having produced a delicacy of feeling. Not
that I have any doubt that sooner or later such feelings
would have grown up spontaneously in the human breast.
The *Æneid* is considerably more *tender* than the *Iliad*.

The theory held by Jesus was that of the Arab philoso-
phers of His day; the only new thing introduced into the
world as a result of the principles preached by Saint Paul
is a body of priests absolutely set apart from their fellow
citizens and having, indeed, diametrically opposite inter-
ests to theirs.[1]

This body made it its sole business to cultivate and
strengthen the *religious sense;* it invented privileges and
habits to stir the hearts of all classes, from the uncultured
shepherd to the jaded courtier; it contrived to stamp the
memory of itself on the charming impressions of early
childhood; it never allowed the slightest pestilence or gen-
eral calamity to pass without profiting by it to intensify
the dread and *sense of religion,* or at any rate to build a
fine church, like the Salute at Venice.

The existence of this body produced that admirable spec-
tacle: Pope Saint Leo resisting without *physical force* the
savage Attila and his hordes of barbarians who had just
overrun China, Persia and the Gauls.

[1] See Montesquieu, *Politique des Romains dans la religion.*

[5]

And so, religion, like that absolute power tempered by popular songs, which we call the French Monarchy, has produced certain singular things which the world might never, perhaps, have seen had it been deprived of those two institutions.

Among these several things, good or bad but all alike singular and curious, which would indeed have astonished Aristotle, Polybius, Augustus, and the other wise heads of antiquity, I have no hesitation in including the wholly modern character of Don Juan. He is, to my mind, a product of the *ascetic institutions* of the Popes that came after Luther; for Leo X and his court (1506) followed more or less closely the religious principles of the Athenians.

Molière's Don Juan was performed early in the reign of Louis XIV, on the 15th of February, 1665; that monarch was not as yet devout, nevertheless the ecclesiastical censure ordered the scene of the *beggar in the forest* to be omitted. These censors, to strengthen their positon, tried to persuade the young king, so prodigiously ignorant, that the word Jansenist was synonymous with Republican.[1]

The original is by a Spaniard, Tirso de Molina;[2] an Italian company played an imitation of it in Paris about the year 1664, and created a furore. It has probably been acted more often than any other comedy in the world. This is because it contains the devil and love, the fear of hell and an exalted passion for a woman, that is to say the most terrible and the most attractive things that exist

---

[1] Saint-Simon, *Mémoires de l'abbé Blache.*

[2] This was the name adopted by a monk, a man of parts, Fray Gabriel Tellez. He belonged to the Order of Mercy, and we have several plays by him in which there are inspired passages, among others *El Timido á la Corte.* Tellez was the author of three hundred comedies, some seventy or eighty of which still survive. He died about 1610.

in the eyes of all men who have to any degree risen above the level of savagery.

It is not surprising that the portrait of Don Juan was introduced into literature by a Spanish poet. Love fills a large place in the life of that nation; it is a serious passion there, and one that compels the sacrifice of every other passion to itself, including that, incredible as it may seem, of *vanity!* It is the same in Germany and in Italy. Properly speaking, France is the only country completely free from this passion, which makes these foreigners commit so many acts of folly: such as marrying a penniless girl, making the excuse that she is pretty and you are in love with her. Girls who lack beauty do not lack admirers in France; we are a cautious people. Otherwise they are reduced to entering religion, and that is why convents are indispensable in Spain. Girls have no dowry in that country, and this rule has maintained the triumph of love. In France has not love fled to the attics, taken refuge, that is, among the girls who do not marry by the intervention of the family lawyer?

Nothing need be said of the Don Juan of Lord Byron, he is merely a Faublas, a good looking but insignificant young man, upon whom all sorts of improbable good fortune are heaped.

So it is in Italy alone, and there only in the sixteenth century that this singular character could make his first appearance. It was in Italy and in the seventeenth century that a Princess said, as she sipped an ice with keen enjoyment on the evening of a hot day: *"What a pity, this is not a sin!"*

This sentiment forms, in my opinion, the foundation of the character of a Don Juan, and, as we see, the Christian religion is necessary to it.

As to which a Neapolitan writer exclaims: "Is it nothing to defy heaven, and to believe that at that very instant heaven may consume one to ashes? Hence, it is said, the intense pleasure of having a nun for one's mistress, and a nun full of piety, who knows quite well that she is doing wrong, and asks pardon of God with passion, as she sins with passion." [1]

Let us take the case of a Christian extremely perverse, born in Rome at the moment when the stern Pius V had just restored to favour or invented a mass of trifling practices absolutely alien to that simple morality which gives the name of virtue only to *what is of use to mankind*. An inexorable Inquisition, so inexorable indeed that it lasted but a short time in Italy, and was obliged to take refuge in Spain, had been given fresh powers,[2] and was inspiring terror in all. For some years, the severest penalties were attached to the non-observance or public disparagement of these minute little practices, raised to the rank of the most sacred duties of religion; the perverse Roman of whom we have spoken would have shrugged his shoulders when he saw the whole of his fellow citizens trembling before the terrible laws of the Inquisition.

"Very good!" we can imagine him saying to himself, "I am the richest man in Rome, this capital of the world; I am going to be the most courageous man also; I shall publicly deride everything that these people respect, and

[1] Don Domenico Paglietta.

[2] Saint Pius V (Ghislieri), a Piedmontese, whose thin, stern face is to be seen on the tomb of Sixtus V in Santa Maria Maggiore, was *Grand Inquisitor* when he was called to the throne of Saint Peter, in 1586. He governed the Church for six years and twenty-four days. The reader should refer to his letters, edited by M. de Potter, the only man of our time with any knowledge of this detail of history. The work of M. de Potter, an inexhaustible mine of facts, is the fruit of fourteen years of conscientious research in the libraries of Florence, Venice and Rome.

that bears so little resemblance to what people ought to respect."

For a Don Juan, to be true to his type, must be a man of feeling, and be endowed with that quick and keen mind which gives one a clear insight into the motives of human actions.

Francesco Cenci must have said to himself: "By what speaking actions can I, a Roman, born in Rome in the year 1527, during those six months in which the Lutheran troops of the Connétable de Bourbon were committing the most appalling profanations in the holy places; by what actions can I call attention to my own courage and give myself, as fully as possible, the pleasure of defying public opinion? How am I to astonish my foolish contemporaries? How can I give myself that keenest of pleasures, of feeling myself to be different from all that vulgar rabble?"

It could never have entered the head of a Roman, and of a Roman of those days to stop short at words. There is no country in which brave words are more despised than Italy.

The man who might have conversed thus with himself was called Francesco Cenci: he was killed before the eyes of his wife and daughter on the 15th of September, 1598. No pleasant memories remain to us of this Don Juan, his character was in no way softened and *modified,* like that of Molière's Don Juan, by the idea of being, first and foremost, a man of the world. He paid no heed to the rest of mankind except by shewing his superiority to them, making use of them in carrying out his plans, or hating them. For your Don Juan finds no pleasure in sympathy, in sweet musings or in the illusions of a tender heart. He requires, above all, pleasures which shall be triumphs, which can be seen by others, and *cannot be denied;* he requires the list flaunted by the insolent Leporello before the sorrowful eyes of Elvira.

[9]

The Roman Don Juan took good care to avoid the signal folly of giving the key to his character and confiding his secrets to a lackey, like the Don Juan of Molière; he lived without a confidant, and uttered no words save those that would be useful in the *advancement of his projects*. No one ever surprised him in one of those moments of true tenderness and charming gaiety which make us forgive the Don Juan of Mozart; in short, the portrait which I am about to reproduce is appalling.

Had I been free to choose, I should not have written of this character, I should have confined myself to studying it, for it is more horrible than strange; but I must explain that it was demanded of me by travelling companions to whom I could refuse nothing. In 1823 I had the pleasure of visiting Italy with certain charming people, whom I shall never forget; like them, I was captivated by the portrait of Beatrice Cenci which is to be seen in Rome, at the palazzo Barberini.

The gallery of that palazzo is now reduced to seven or eight pictures; but of these four are masterpieces: there is first of all the portrait of the famous *Fornarina,* Raphael's mistress, by Raphael himself. This portrait, of the authenticity of which no doubt can be entertained, for we find copies of it made at the time, differs entirely from the figure which, in the gallery at Florence, is described as that of Raphael's mistress, and has been engraved, with that title, by Morghen. The Florence portrait is not even by Raphael. In deference to that great name, will the reader kindly pardon this little digression?

The second priceless portrait in the Barberini gallery is by Guido; it is the portrait of Beatrice Cenci, of which one sees so many bad engravings. That great painter has placed a meaningless piece of drapery over Beatrice's throat: he has crowned her with a turban; he would have been afraid of carrying accuracy to the pitch of horror had he reproduced exactly the toilet that she made before appearing at the place of execution, and the dishevelled hair of a poor girl of sixteen, abandoned to the wildest despair. The face has sweetness and beauty, the expression is most appealing and the eyes very large: they have the startled air of a person who has just been caught in the act of shedding large tears. The hair is golden and of great beauty. This head has nothing of the Roman pride and consciousness of its own strength which one often detects in the assured glance of a daughter of the Tiber, *una figlia del Tevere, as they say of themselves with pride.* Unfortunately the flesh tints of this portrait have turned to *brick red* during the long interval of two hundred and thirty-eight years which separates us from the catastrophe of which you are about to read.

The third portrait in the Barberini gallery is that of Lucrezia Petroni, Beatrice's stepmother, who was executed with her. She is the type of the Roman matron in her natural beauty and pride.[1] The features are large and the flesh of a dazzling whiteness, the eyebrows are black and strongly marked, the gaze commanding and at the same time sensuous. She makes a fine contrast with so sweet, so simple a face, almost a German face, as that of her stepdaughter.

The fourth portrait, rendered striking by the accuracy and brightness of its colouring, is one of the masterpieces of Titian; it is that of a Greek slave who was the mistress of the famous Doge Barbarigo.

Almost invariably, foreigners coming to Rome ask to be taken, at the outset of their tour of inspection, to the Barberini gallery; they are attracted, the women especially, by the portraits of Beatrice Cenci and her stepmother. I had my share of the general curiosity; then,

---

[1] This pride is not in the least dependent on social *rank,* as in portraits by Vandyck.

like everyone else, I sought to obtain access to the reports of the famous trial. If you are similarly privileged, you will be quite surprised, I expect, as you peruse these documents, which are all in Latin except the replies made by the accused persons, to find almost no indication of the facts of the case. The reason is that in Rome, in 1599, there was no one who was not acquainted with the facts. I purchased the right to transcribe a contemporary account; I felt that it would be possible to give a translation of it without shocking any sensibility; anyhow this translation could be read aloud before ladies in 1823. It must be understood that the translator ceases to be faithful to his original when he can no longer be so: otherwise the sense of horror would soon outweigh that of curiosity.

The tragic part played by a Don Juan (one who seeks to conform to no ideal standard, and considers public opinion only with a view to outraging it) is here set forth in all its horror. The enormity of his crimes forces two unhappy women to have him killed before their eyes; of these two women one was his wife and the other his daughter, and the reader will not dare to make up his mind as to whether they were guilty. Their contemporaries were of the opinion that they ought not to have been put to death.

I am convinced that the tragedy of *Galeotto Manfredl* (who was killed by his wife: the subject is treated by the great poet Monti) and ever so many other domestic tragedies of the *cinquecento,* which are less well known, and barely mentioned in the local histories of Italian cities, ended in a scene similar to that in the castle of Petrella. What follows is my translation of the contemporary account; it is in the *Italian of Rome,* and was written on the 14th of September, 1599.

THE CENCI

A TRUE NARRATIVE

**Of the deaths of Giacomo and Beatrice Cenci,
and of Lucrezia Petroni Cenci, their step-
mother, executed for the crime of parricide,
on Saturday last, the 11th of September,
1599, in the reign of our Holy Father the
Pope, Clement VIII, Aldobrandini.**

THE execrable life consistently led by Francesco Cenci,
a native of Rome and one of the wealthiest of our fellow
citizens, has ended by leading him to disaster. He has
brought to a precocious death his sons, stout hearted young
fellows, and his daughter Beatrice, who, although she
mounted the scaffold when barely sixteen years old (four
days since), was reckoned nevertheless one of the chief
beauties of the States of the Church, if not the whole of
Italy. The rumour has gone abroad that Signor Guido
Reni, one of the pupils of that admirable school of
Bologna, was pleased to paint the portrait of poor Beatrice,
last Friday, that is to say on the day preceding her execu-
tion. If this great painter has performed this task as he
has done in the case of the other paintings which he has
executed in this capital, posterity will be able to form
some idea of the beauty of this lovely girl. In order
that it may also preserve some record of her unprecedented
misfortunes, and of the astounding force with which this
truly Roman nature was able to fight against them, I have
decided to write down what I have learned as to the action
which brought her to her death, and what I saw on the day
of her glorious tragedy.

The people who have supplied me with my information
were in a position which made them acquainted with the
most secret details, such as are unknown in Rome even

to-day, although for the last six weeks people have been speaking of nothing but the Cenci trial. I shall write with a certain freedom, knowing as I do that I shall be able to deposit my *commentary* in respectable archives from which it will certainly not be released until after my day. My one regret is that I must pronounce, but truth will have it so, against the innocence of this poor Beatrice Cenci, as greatly adored and respected by all that knew her as her horrible father was hated and execrated.

This man who, indisputably, had received from heaven the most astounding sagacity and eccentricity, was the son of Monsignor Cenci, who, under Pius V, had risen to the post of *Tesoriere*, or Minister of Finance. That saintly Pope, entirely taken up, as we know, with his righteous hatred of heresy and the re-establishment of his admirable Inquisition, felt only contempt for the temporal administration of his State, so that this Monsignor Cenci, who was Treasurer for some years before 1572, found himself able to leave to this terrible man who was his son and the father of Beatrice Cenci a clear income of one hundred and sixty thousand piastres (about two and a half millions of our francs in 1837).

Francesco Cenci, apart from this great fortune, had a reputation for courage and prudence to which, in his youth, no other Roman could lay claim; and this reputation established him all the more firmly at the Papal court and among the people as a whole, inasmuch as the criminal actions which were beginning to be imputed to him were all of the kind which the world is most ready to forgive. Many citizens of Rome still recalled, with a bitter regret, the freedom of thought and action which they had enjoyed in the days of Leo X, who was taken from us in 1513, and under Paul III, who died in 1549. Already, in the reign of the latter of these Popes, people were beginning

to speak of young Francesco Cenci on account of certain
singular love affairs, carried to a successful issue by means
more singular still.

Under Paul III, at a time when one could still speak
with a certain degree of freedom, many people said that
Francesco delighted most of all in strange incidents such
as might give him *peripezie di nuova idea,* novel and dis-
turbing sensations; those who take this view find support
in the discovery, among his account books, of such entries
as the following:

"For the adventuros and *peripezie* of Toscanella, three
thousand five hundred piastres" (about sixty thousand
francs in 1837) *"e non fu caro"* (and not dear at that).

It is not known, perhaps, in the other cities of Italy,
that our destinies and our mode of conduct in Rome vary
with the character of the reigning Pope. Thus, for thir-
teen years, under the good Pope Gregory XIII (Buon-
compagni), everything was permitted in Rome; if you
wished, you had your enemy stabbed, and were never pun-
ished, provided that you behaved in a modest fashion.
This excessive indulgence was followed by an excessive
severity during the five years of the reign of the great
Sixtus V, of whom it has been said, as of the Emperor
Augustus, that he should either never have occurred or
have remained for ever. Then one saw wretched creatures
executed for murders or poisonings which had been for-
gotten for ten years, but which they had been so unfor-
tunate as to confess to Cardinal Montalto, afterwards
Sixtus V.

It was chiefly under Gregory XIII that people began
to speak regularly of Francesco Cenci; he had married a
wife of great wealth and such as befitted a gentleman of
his high standing; she died after bearing him seven chil-
dren. Shortly after her death, he took as his second wife
Lucrezia Petroni, a woman of rare beauty, and distin-

guished especially for the dazzling whiteness of her skin, but a little too plump, a common fault among our Roman women. By Lucrezia he had no children.

The least fault to be found with Francesco Cenci was his propensity towards an infamous form of love; the greatest was that of unbelief in God. Never in his life was he seen to enter a church.

Three times imprisoned for his infamous love affairs, he secured his freedom by giving two hundred thousand piastres to the persons most in favour with the twelve successive Popes under whom he lived. (Two hundred thousand piastres amount to about five millions in 1837.)

When I first set eyes on Francesco Cenci his hair was already grey, during the reign of Pope Buoncompagni, when every licence was allowed to such as dared take it. He was a man of about five feet four inches, and very well built, though a trifle thin; he was reputed to be extremely strong, possibly he spread this rumour himself; he had large and expressive eyes, but the upper lids were too much inclined to droop; his nose was too large and prominent, his lips thin, and parted in a charming smile. This smile became terrible when he fastened his gaze on one of his enemies; if anything moved or annoyed him, he would begin to tremble in an alarming fashion. I have known him when I was young, in the days of Pope Buoncompagni, go on horseback from Rome to Naples, doubtless upon some amorous errand; he would pass through the forests of San Germano and la Faggiola, regardless of brigands, and would complete the journey, it was said, in less than twenty hours. He travelled always by himself, and without informing anyone; when his first horse was worn out, he would buy or steal another. Should any objection be offered by the owner, he had no objection, himself, to using his dagger. But it is true to say that in the days of my youth, that is to say when he was about forty-eight or fifty, there was no one bold enough to withstand him. His great pleasure was to defy his enemies.

He was very well known on all the roads in the States of His Holiness; he paid generously, but he was capable also, two or three months after an injury had been done him, of sending one of his *sicarj* to dispatch the person who had offended him.

The one virtuous action which he performed in the whole of his long life was to build, in the courtyard of his vast palazzo by the Tiber, a church dedicated to Saint Thomas; and even to this good deed he was prompted by the curious desire to be able to look down [1] upon the graves of all his children, whom he hated with an extravagant and unnatural loathing, even in their earliest infancy, when they were incapable of offending him in any way.

"That is where I wish to put them all," he would often say with a bitter laugh to the masons whom he employed to build his church. He sent the three eldest, Giacomo, Cristoforo and Rocco, to study at the University of Salamanca in Spain. Once they were in that distant land he took an evil delight in never sending them any money, so that these unfortunate youths, after addressing a number of letters to their father, who made no reply, were reduced to the miserable necessity, for their return journey, of borrowing small sums of money or begging their way along the roads.

In Rome, they found a father more severe and rigid, more harsh than ever, who, for all his immense wealth, would neither clothe them nor give them the money necessary to purchase the cheapest forms of food. They were obliged to have recourse to the Pope, who forced Francesco Cenci to make them a small allowance. With this very modest provision they parted from their father.

[1] In Rome people are buried beneath the floors of churches.

Shortly afterwards, on account of some scandalous love affair, Francesco was put in prison for the third and last time; whereupon the three brothers begged an audience of our Holy Father the Pope now reigning, and jointly besought him to put to death Francesco Cenci their father, who, they said, was dishonouring their house. Clement VIII had a great mind to do so, but decided not to follow his first impulse, so as not to give satisfaction to these unnatural children, and expelled them ignominiously from his presence.

The father, as we have already said, came out of prison after paying a large sum of money to a powerful protector. It may be imagined that the strange action of his three elder sons was bound to increase still further the hatred that he felt for his children. He continually rained curses on them all, old and young, and every day would take a stick to his two poor daughters, who lived with him in his palazzo.

The eldest daughter, although closely watched, by dint of endless efforts managed to present a petition to the Pope; she implored His Holiness to give her in marriage or to place her in a convent. Clement VIII took pity on her distress, and married her to Carlo Gabrielli, of the noblest family of Gubbio; His Holiness obliged her father to give her an ample dowry.

Struck by this unexpected blow, Francesco Cenci shewed an intense rage, and to prevent Beatrice, when she grew older, from taking it into her head to follow her sister's example, confined her in one of the apartments of his huge palazzo. There, no one was allowed to set eyes on Beatrice, at that time barely fourteen years old, and already in the full splendour of her enchanting beauty. She had, above all, a gaiety, a candour and a comic spirit which I have never seen in anyone but her. Francesco Cenci carried her food to her himself. We may suppose that it was then

that the monster fell in love with her, or pretended to fall
in love, in order to torment his wretched daughter. He
often spoke to her of the perfidious trick which her elder
sister had played on him, and flying into a rage at the sound
of his own voice, would end by showering blows on Beatrice.
While this was happening, Rocco Cenci, his son, was
killed by a pork-butcher, and, in the following year, Cristo-
foro Cenci was killed by Paolo Corso of Massa. On this
occasion, he displayed his black impiety, for at the funerals
of his two sons he refused to spend so much as a single
baiocco on candles. On learning of the death of his son
Cristoforo, he exclaimed that he could never be truly happy
until all his children were buried, and that, when the last
of them died, he would, as a sign of joy, set fire to his
palazzo. Rome was astounded at this utterance, but con-
sidered that everything was possible with such a man, who
gloried in defying the whole world, including the Pope
himself.

(Here it becomes quite impossible to follow the Roman
narrator in his extremely obscure account of the strange
actions by which Francesco Cenci sought to astonish his
contemporaries. His wife and his unfortunate daughter
were, to all appearance, made the victims of his abominable
ideas.)

All this was not enough for him; he attempted with
threats, and with the use of force, to outrage his own
daughter Beatrice, who was already fully grown and beau-
tiful; he was not ashamed to go and lie down in her bed,
being himself completely naked. He walked about with
her in the rooms of his palazzo, still stark naked; then he
took her into his wife's bed, in order that, by the light of
the lamps, poor Lucrezia might see what he was doing to
Beatrice.

He taught the poor girl a frightful heresy, which I
scarcely dare repeat, to wit that, when a father has carnal

knowledge of his own daughter, the children born of the union are of necessity saints, and that all the greatest saints whom the Church venerates were born in this manner, that is to say, that their maternal grandfather was also their father.

When Beatrice resisted his execrable intentions, he belaboured her with the cruellest blows, until the wretched girl, unable to endure so miserable an existence, decided to follow the example that her sister had given her. She addressed to our Holy Father the Pope a petition set forth in great detail; but there is reason to believe that Francesco Cenci had taken due precautions, for it does not appear that this petition ever came into the hands of His Holiness; at least, it could not be found in the secretariat of the *Memoriali,* when, after Beatrice's imprisonment, her counsel was in urgent need of the document; it would to some extent have furnished proof of the appalling excesses committed in the castle of la Petrella. Would it not have been evident to all that Beatrice Cenci had found herself legally entitled to protection? This memorial was written also in the name of Lucrezia, Beatrice's stepmother.

Francesco Cenci learned of this attempt, and one may guess with what fury he intensified his maltreatment of these two wretched women.

Life became absolutely intolerable to them, and it was at this point that, seeing that they had nothing to expect from the justice of the Sovereign, whose courtiers were seduced by Francesco's lavish gifts, they conceived the idea of adopting those extreme measures which ended in their ruin, but had nevertheless the advantage of ending their sufferings in this world.

It should be explained that the famous Monsignor Guerra was a frequent visitor to the palazzo Cenci; he was a man of tall stature and extremely handsome to boot, and had received this special gift from fortune that, to whatever task he might apply himself, he performed it with a grace that was quite peculiarly his own. It has been supposed that he was in love with Beatrice and had thoughts of discarding the *mantellata* and marrying her; [1] but, albeit he took the utmost care to conceal his feelings, he was execrated by Francesco Cenci, who accused him of having been the intimate friend of all his children. When Monsignor Guerra knew that Signor Cenci was not in his palazzo, he went up to the ladies' rooms, and spent several hours in conversing with them and listening to their complaints of the incredible treatment to which they were both subjected. It appears that Beatrice was the first to speak openly to Monsignor Guerra of the plan upon which they had decided. After a time, he promised them his support; and finally, after strong and repeated pressure from Beatrice, consented to convey their strange design to Giacomo Cenci, without whose consent nothing could be done, since he was the eldest brother, and head of the family after Francesco.

Nothing was easier than to draw him into the conspiracy; he was treated extremely ill by his father, who gave him no assistance, a deprivation which Giacomo felt all the more keenly, inasmuch as he was married and had six children. The conspirators chose as a meeting place, in which to discuss the means of putting Francesco Cenci to death, Monsignor Guerra's apartment. They conducted their business with due formality, and the votes of the stepmother and the girl were taken on all points. When at length a decision had been reached, they chose two of Francesco Cenci's vassals, each of whom had conceived an undying hatred for him. One of these was named Marzio; he was a stout fellow, deeply attached to Francesco's unfortunate children, and, in order to do something that would

[1] The majority of the *monsignori* are not in holy orders, and are free to marry.

give them pleasure, he consented to take part in the parricide. Olimpio, the second, had been chosen as warden of the fortress of la Petrella, in the Kingdom of Naples, by Prince Colonna; but, by using his all-powerful influence with the Prince, Francesco Cenci had procured his dismissal.

Everything was arranged with these two men; Francesco Cenci having announced that, in order to escape from the unhealthy air of Rome, he was going to spend the summer in this fortress of la Petrella, it occurred to them that they might collect there a dozen Neapolitan *banditi*. Olimpio undertook to provide these. It was decided to conceal the men in the forests adjoining la Petrella, to warn them of the hour at which Francesco Cenci was to start on his journey; they would intercept him on the road, and send word to his family that they would release him on payment of a large ransom. Then his children would be obliged to return to Rome to collect the sum demanded by the brigands; they would pretend to be unable to find this sum immediately, and the brigands, carrying out their threat, and seeing no sign of the money, would put Francesco Cenci to death. In this way, no one would be led to suspect the true authors of the crime.

But, when summer came and Francesco Cenci left Rome for la Petrella, the spy who was to give notice that he had started was too late in warning the *banditi* posted in the woods, and they had not time to come down to the high road. Cenci arrived without interference at la Petrella; the brigands, tired of waiting for an uncertain booty, went off to rob elsewhere on their own account.

For his part, Cenci, grown prudent and cautious with advancing years, never ventured to emerge from his fortress. And, his ill humour increasing with the infirmities of age, which he found insupportable, he intensified the atrocious treatment which he made the two poor women undergo. He pretended that they were rejoicing in his weakness.

Beatrice, driven to desperation by the horrible things which she had to endure, summoned Marzio and Olimpio beneath the walls of the fortress. During the night, while her father slept, she conversed with them from one of the lower windows and threw down to them letters addressed to Monsignor Guerra. By means of these letters, it was arranged that Monsignor Guerra should promise Marzio and Olimpio a thousand piastres if they would take upon themselves the responsibility for putting Francesco Cenci to death. A third of the sum was to be paid in Rome, before the deed, by Monsignor Guerra, and the other two-thirds by Lucrezia and Beatrice, when, the deed done, they should be in command of Cenci's strong-box.

It was further agreed that the deed should be done on the Nativity of the Virgin, and for this purpose the two men were secretly admitted to the fortress. But Lucrezia was overcome by the respect due to a festival of the Madonna, and she made Beatrice postpone the action until the following day, so as not to be guilty of a twofold crime.

It was therefore on the evening of the 9th of September, 1598, that, mother and daughter having with great dexterity administered opium to Francesco Cenci, that man so hard to deceive, he fell into a deep sleep.

Towards midnight Beatrice herself let into the fortress Marzio and Olimpio; next, Lucrezia and Beatrice led them to the old man's room, where he lay fast asleep. There, they were left by themselves that they might do what had been determined upon, and the women withdrew to wait in an adjoining room. Suddenly they saw the two men appear with pallid faces, and apparently out of their wits.

"What has happened?" cried the ladies.

"It is a shame and a disgrace," the men answered, "to kill a poor old man in his sleep! Pity stayed our hands."

On hearing this excuse, Beatrice grew indignant, and
began to abuse them, saying:

"And so you two men, thoroughly prepared to act, have
not the courage to kill a man in his sleep! [1] You would
be a great deal less willing to look him in the face if he
were awake! And so it is for nothing more than this that
you dare to ask for money? Very well! Since your cow-
ardice forces me, I will kill my father myself; and as for
you, you have not long to live either!"

Animated by these few scathing words, and fearing a
reduction of the fee that had been promised them, the
assassins boldly returned to the bedroom, followed by the
women. One of them had a great nail which he placed
vertically over the sleeping man's eye; the other, who had
a hammer, drove the nail into his head. Another large nail
was driven similarly into his breast, so that the wretched
soul, burdened with all its recent sins, was carried off by
devils; the body struggled, but in vain.

The deed accomplished, the girl gave Olimpio a great
purse filled with money: she gave Marzio a cloak of broad-
cloth with a gold stripe, which had belonged to her father,
and dismissed them.

The women, left to themselves, began by withdrawing
the large nail driven into the head of the corpse, and the
other in his throat; then, after wrapping the body in a
sheet from the bed, they dragged it through a long series
of rooms to a gallery which overlooked a small, deserted
garden. From this gallery, they threw down the body upon
a great elder tree which grew in that lonely spot. As there
was a privy at the end of this little gallery, they hoped
that when, in the morning, the old man's body was found
caught in the branches of the elder, it would be supposed

---

[1] All these details were proved at the trial.

that his foot had slipped and that he had fallen while on his way to the privy.

Things fell out exactly as they had foreseen. In the morning, when the body was found, a great clamour arose in the fortress; they did not forget to utter piercing cries, and to bewail the lamentable death of their husband and father. But the young Beatrice had the courage of outraged modesty, not the prudence necessary in this life; early in the morning, she had given to a woman who washed the linen in the fortress a sheet stained with blood, telling her not to be surprised at such a quantity of blood, because she herself, all night long, had been suffering from a copious issue, and in this way, for the moment, all went well.

Francesco Cenci was given a pompous funeral, and the women returned to Rome to enjoy that tranquillity which they had for so long desired in vain. They imagined themselves to be happy now for ever, for they did not know what was happening at Naples.

The justice of heaven, which would not allow so atrocious a parricide to remain unpunished, brought it about that, as soon as the news reached that city of what had occurred in the fortress of la Petrella, the principal judge there felt misgivings, and sent a royal commissioner to examine the body and arrest any suspected persons.

The royal commissioner ordered the arrest of everyone living in the fortress. They were all taken to Naples in chains; and nothing in their depositions appeared suspicious, except that the laundress professed to have received from Beatrice a sheet or sheets stained with blood. She was asked whether Beatrice had attempted to explain these great stains of blood; she replied that Beatrice had spoken of a natural infirmity. She was asked whether stains of such a size could be due to such an infirmity;

she replied that they could not, and that the stains on the sheet were of too bright a red.

This information was immediately sent to the judicial authorities in Rome, and yet many months elapsed before it occurred to anyone here to order the arrest of Francesco Cenci's children. Lucrezia, Beatrice and Giacomo could have escaped a thousand times over, either by going to Florence on the pretext of making some pilgrimage, or by taking ship at Civita-Vecchia; but God withheld from them this life-giving inspiration.

Monsignor Guerra, having had word of what was happening in Naples, at once sent out a number of men with orders to kill Marzio and Olimpio; but Olimpio alone did they succeed in killing at Terni. The Neapolitan authorities had arrested Marzio, who was taken to Naples, where he immediately confessed all.

This terrible deposition was at once sent to the authorities in Rome, who at last decided to arrest and confine in the Corte Savella prison Giacomo and Bernardo Cenci, the only surviving sons of Francesco, as also Lucrezia, his widow. Beatrice was guarded in her father's palazzo by a numerous troop of *sbirri*. Marzio was brought from Naples, and likewise confined in the Savella prison; there he was confronted with the two women, who denied everything consistently, Beatrice in particular refusing steadfastly to recognise the striped cloak which she had given to Marzio. The brigand, overcome by enthusiasm for the marvellous beauty and astonishing eloquence of the girl as she answered the judge, denied everything that he had confessed in Naples. He was put to the question, he admitted nothing, preferring to die in agony; fit homage to the beauty of Beatrice!

After the death of this man, there being no proof of the crime, the judges found that there was not sufficient reason for putting to the torture either Cenci's two sons or the two women. All four were taken to the Castel Sant' Angelo, where they remained for some months in peace and quietness.

The matter seemed to be at an end, and no one in Rome had any doubt that this girl, of such beauty and courage, who had aroused so keen an interest, would shortly be set at liberty, when, unfortunately, the officers of justice succeeded in arresting the brigand who, at Terni, had killed Ulimpio; he was brought to Rome, where he confessed everything.

Monsignor Guerra, whom the brigand's confession so dangerously compromised, was summoned to appear before the court without delay; imprisonment was certain, death probable. But this remarkable man, whom fate had endowed with the art of doing everything well, succeeded in escaping in a manner which seems miraculous. He was reckoned the handsomest man at the Papal court, and was too well known in Rome to have any chance of escape; besides, a close watch was being kept at the gates, and probably, from the moment of his summons, his house had been under supervision. It should be added that he was very tall, with an extremely fair skin, and a fine beard and hair, fair also.

With inconceivable rapidity, he procured a charcoal seller, took his clothes, had his own head and beard shaved, stained his face, bought a pair of asses, and began to perambulate the streets of Rome selling charcoal, limping as he went. He assumed with admirable skill an air of plebeian stupidity, and went about crying his charcoal with his mouth full of bread and onions, while hundreds of *sbirri* were searching for him not only in Rome, but on all the roads as well. At length, when his appearance was familiar to most of the *sbirri,* he ventured to leave Rome, still driving before him his pair of asses laden with charcoal. He met several troops of *sbirri,* who had no thought of stopping him. Since then, only one letter has been received from him; his mother has sent money to him at Marseilles, and it is supposed that he is serving in the French war, as a private soldier.

The confession of the Terni assassin and this flight of Monsignor Guerra, which created an enormous sensation in Rome, so revived suspicion, and indeed seemed so to point to the guilt of the Cenci, that they were taken from the Castel Sant' Angelo and brought back to the Savella prison.

The two brothers, put to the torture, were far from imitating the magnanimity of the brigand Marzio; they were so pusillanimous as to confess everything. Signora Lucrezia Petroni was so habituated to the ease and comfort of a life of the greatest luxury, and besides was so stout in figure that she could not endure the question by the *cord;* she told everything that she knew.

But it was not so with Beatrice Cenci, a girl full of vivacity and courage. Neither the kind words nor the threats of the judge Moscati had any effect on her. She endured the torture of the *cord* without a moment's faltering and with perfect courage. Never once could the judge induce her to give an answer that compromised her in the slightest degree; indeed, by her quick-witted vivacity, she utterly confounded the famous Ulisse Moscati, the judge responsible for examining her. He was so much surprised by the conduct of the girl that he felt it his duty to make a full report to His Holiness Pope Clement VIII, whom God preserve.

His Holiness wished to see the documents and to study the case. He was afraid lest the judge Ulisse Moscati, so celebrated for his deep learning and the superior sagacity of his mind, might have been overpowered by Beatrice's beauty, and be helping her out in his examinations of her. The consequence was that His Holiness took the case out of his hands, and entrusted it to another and a more severe judge. Indeed, this barbarian had the heart to subject without pity so lovely a body *ad torturam capillorum* (that is to say, questions were put to Beatrice Cenci while she was hanging by her hair[1]).

While she was fastened to the cord, this new judge confronted Beatrice with her stepmother and her brothers. As soon as Giacomo and Donna Lucrezia saw her:

"The sin has been committed," they cried; "you should perform the ponance also, and not let your body be torn to pieces through a futile obstinacy."

"So you wish to cover our house with shame," replied the girl, "and to die an ignominious death. You are greatly mistaken; but, since you wish it, so be it."

And, turning to the *sbirri:*

"Release me," she said to them, "and let someone read over to me my mother's examination. I will admit what must be admitted, and deny what must be denied."

This was duly done; she admitted everything that was true.[2] Immediately the chains were removed from them all, and because for five months she had not seen her brothers, she expressed a wish to dine with them, and all four spent a very happy day together.

But next day they were separated once more; the two brothers were taken to the prison of Tordinona, while the women remained in the Savella. Our Holy Father the Pope, having seen the authentic document containing all their confessions, ordered that without further delay they

[1] See the treatise *de Suppliciis*, by the celebrated Farinacci, a jurist of the time. It contains horrible details which our nineteenth century sensibility cannot endure even to read about, but which were very creditably endured by a Roman girl of sixteen abandoned by her lover.

[2] Farinacci quotes several passages from Beatrice's confession; they seem to me touching in their simplicity.

should be tied to the tails of wild horses, and so put to death.

The whole of Rome shuddered on learning of this rigorous decree. A great number of cardinals and princes went to throw themselves on their knees before the Pope, imploring him to allow the poor wretches to present their defence.

"And they, did they give their aged father time to present his?" the Pope replied angrily.

Finally, by a special grace, he was pleased to allow a respite of five and twenty days. At once the leading *avvocati* in Rome began to write their pleadings in this case which had filled the town with pity and dismay. On the twenty-fifth day, they appeared in a body before His Holiness. Niccolò de' Angelis was the first to speak, but he had barely read the first line of his defence when Clement VIII interrupted him:

"And so, here in Rome," he exclaimed, "we find people who kill their father, and counsel afterwards to defend such people!"

All stood speechless, until Farinacci ventured to raise his voice.

"Most Holy Father," he said, "we are here not to defend the crime, but to prove, if we can, that one or more of these unfortunate people are innocent of the crime."

The Pope made a sign to him to speak, and he spoke for fully three hours, after which the Pope took their briefs from them all and dismissed them. As they were leaving the presence, Altieri was the last to go; he was afraid that he might have compromised himself, and turned to kneel before the Pope, saying:

"I could not help appearing in this case, since I am counsel for the poor."

To which the Pope replied:

"We are not surprised at you, but at the others."

The Pope refused to go to bed, but spent the whole night reading the pleadings of counsel, calling upon the Cardinal of San Marcello to help him in this task; His Holiness appeared so deeply touched that many people felt a spark of hope for the lives of the unhappy prisoners. In the hope of saving the sons, the counsel threw the whole onus of the crime upon Beatrice. As it had been proved in the trial that her father had on several occasions employed force with a criminal intention, the lawyers hoped that the murder would be pardoned in her case, as being justified in self-defence; and if so, when the principal author of the crime was granted her life, how could her brothers, who had acted at her persuasion, be put to death?

After this night devoted to his judicial duties, Clement VIII ordered that the accused persons should be taken back to prison and placed in *secret confinement*. This circumstance gave rise to great hopes in Rome, which throughout the whole of this case considered no one but Beatrice. It was alleged that she had been in love with Monsignor Guerra, but that she had never infringed the rules of the strictest virtue; it was impossible, therefore, in justice, to impute to her the crimes of a monster, and she was to be punished because she had made use of her right of self-defence; what would have been her punishment had she consented? Was it necessary that human justice should step in to increase the misery of a creature so lovable, so deserving of pity, and already in such a plight? After so sad a life, which had heaped upon her every form of misery before her sixteenth birthday, had she not acquired the right to a few days of greater happiness? The whole of Rome seemed to be briefed in her defence. Would she not have been pardoned if, when for the first time Francesco Cenci made a criminal assault upon her, she had stabbed him?

Pope Clement VIII was mild and merciful. We were

beginning to hope that, a little ashamed of the burst of ill temper which had made him interrupt the counsels' pleadings, he would pardon one who had repelled force with force, not, to be accurate, at the moment of the original crime, but when the assailant tried to commit it anew. The whole of Rome was on tenterhooks, when the Pope received the news of the violent death of the Marchesa Costanza Santa Croce. Her son, Paolo Santa Croce, had killed the lady in question, who was sixty years old, by stabbing her with his dagger, because she would not bind herself to make him the heir to her whole fortune. The report added that Santa Croce had taken flight, and that there was little or no hope of arresting him. The Pope remembered the fratricide by the Massini, which had occurred quite recently. Appalled by the frequency of these murders of near relatives, His Holiness felt that he would not be entitled to grant a pardon. When he received this fatal report of the Santa Croce murder, the Pope was at the palace of Monte Cavallo, where he was spending the 6th of September, in order to be nearer, next morning, to the Church of Santa Maria degli Angeli, where he was to consecrate as Bishop a German Cardinal.

On the Friday at the twenty-second hour (4 P.M.) he sent for Ferrante Taverna, the Governor of Rome (afterwards made Cardinal, for so singular a reason), and addressed him in the following words:

"We entrust the case of the Cenci to your hands, in order that justice may be done without delay."

The Governor returned to his Palace deeply moved by the order he had received; he at once signed the sentence of death, and convened a congregation to decide upon the method of execution.

On Saturday morning, the 11th of September, 1599, the first gentlemen of Rome, members of the Confraternity of the Confortatori, repaired to the two prisons, that of Corte

Savella, where were Beatrice and her stepmother, and
Tordinona, in which Giacomo and Bernardo Cenci were
confined. Throughout the whole of the night between the
Friday and the Saturday, the Roman nobles who were
aware of what was happening did nothing but hasten from
the palace of Monte Cavallo to those of the principal Car-
dinals, hoping to obtain at least the concession that the
women might be put to death inside the prison, and not
upon an ignominious scaffold; and that mercy be shewn to
the young Bernardo Cenci, who, being only fifteen years
old, could not have been admitted to the secret. The noble
Cardinal Sforza was conspicuous for his zeal during that
fatal night, but albeit so powerful a prince he could obtain
nothing. The Santa Croce crime was a vile crime, com-
mitted for the sake of money, and the crime of Beatrice
Cenci was committed in defence of her honour.

While the most powerful Cardinals were taking such
fruitless pains, Farinacci, our great jurist, actually dared
to make his way into the Pope's presence; face to face with
His Holiness, this remarkable man contrived to stir his
listener's conscience, and at length, by sheer importunity,
wrested from him the life of Bernardo Cenci.

When the Pope made this important utterance, it was
about four o'clock in the morning (of Saturday, the 11th
of September). All night long men had been at work on
the piazza of the Ponte Sant' Angelo preparing the scene
of this cruel tragedy. All the necessary copies of the death
sentence could not, however, be completed before five
o'clock in the morning, so that it was not until six o'clock
that the fatal tidings could be conveyed to the wretched
prisoners, who were peacefully asleep.

The girl, for the first few moments, could not even sum-
mon up strength to put on her clothes. She uttered piercing
and continuous shrieks and gave way uncontrollably to the
most terrible desperation.

[33]

"How is it possible, oh, God," she cried, "that I must die suddenly, like this?"

Lucrezia Petroni, on the other hand, said nothing that was not entirely proper; first of all, she fell on her knees and prayed, then calmly exhorted her daughter to accompany her to the chapel, where they would make preparation together for the great journey from life to death.

These words restored to Beatrice all her calm; just as she had shewn extravagance and want of control at first, so now she was reasonable and wise as soon as her stepmother had summoned up the resources of that noble soul. From that moment she was a mirror of constancy which all Rome admired.

She asked for a notary to draw up her will, which was permitted. She ordered that her body should be taken to San Pietro in Montorio; she left three hundred thousand francs to the Stimate (nuns of the Stigmata of Saint Francis); this sum was to provide dowries for fifty poor girls. This example moved the heart of Donna Lucrezia, who also made her will and ordered her body to be taken to San Giorgio; she left five hundred thousand francs to that church and made other pious bequests.

At eight o'clock they made their confession, heard mass and received the Holy Communion. But, before going to mass, Donna Beatrice reflected that it was not proper to appear on the scaffold, in the sight of the whole populace, in the rich garments which she was wearing. She ordered two gowns, one for herself, one for her mother. These gowns were made like nuns' habits, without ornaments on bosom or shoulders, and gathered only at the wide sleeves. The stepmother's gown was of black cotton; the girl's of blue taffeta, with a large cord fastening it at the waist.

When the gowns were brought, Donna Beatrice, who was on her knees, rose and said to Donna Lucrezia:

"My lady mother, the hour of our passion approaches;

it would be well for us to make ready, to put on these other
clothes, and for the last time to perform the mutual service
of dressing each other."

There had been erected on the Piazza del Ponte Sant'
Angelo a huge scaffold with a block and a *mannaja* (a sort
of guillotine). About the thirteenth hour (eight o'clock in
the morning), the Company of the Misericordia came with
their great crucifix to the gate of the prison. Giacomo
Cenci was the first to emerge; he fell devoutly upon his
knees at the threshold, made his prayer, and kissed the
Sacred Wounds on the crucifix. He was followed by Ber-
nardo Cenci, his young brother, who also had his hands
bound and a little board before his eyes. The crowd was
enormous, and a disturbance arose owing to a basin which
fell from a window almost upon the head of one of the
penitents who was holding a lighted torch by the side of
the banner.

Everyone was gazing at the brothers, when suddenly the
Fiscal of Rome came forward, and said:

"Don Bernardo, Our Sovereign Lord grants you your
life; prepare to accompany your family, and pray to God
for them."

Thereupon his two *confortatori* removed the little board
that covered his eyes. The executioner installed Giacomo
Cenci on the cart and had removed his coat, as he was to
be tortured with the *pincers*. When the executioner came
to Bernardo, he verified the signature on the pardon, un-
bound him, removed his handcuffs, and, as he had no coat,
for he was awaiting the pincers, the executioner set him
on the cart and wrapped him in a rich cloak of broadcloth
striped with gold. (It was said that this was the same
cloak that was given by Beatrice to Marzio after the deed
in the fortress of la Petrella.) The vast crowd that filled
the street, the windows and the roofs, was suddenly stirred;

one heard a deep and sullen murmur, people were beginning to tell one another that the boy had been pardoned.

The intoning of the Psalms began, and the procession moved slowly across the Piazza Navona towards the Savella prison. On reaching the prison gate the banner halted, the two women came out, made an act of adoration at the foot of the holy crucifix and then proceeded on foot, one following the other. They were dressed in the manner already described, the head of each being draped in a great taffeta veil which reached almost to her waist.

Donna Lucrezia, as a widow, wore a black veil and slippers of black velvet without heels, according to custom.

The girl's veil was of blue taffeta, like her dress; she had in addition a great veil of cloth of silver over her shoulders, a petticoat of violet cloth, and slippers of white velvet, elegantly laced and fastened with crimson cords. She appeared singularly charming as she walked, in this costume, and a tear came to every eye as the spectators caught sight of her slowly advancing in the rear of the procession.

Both women had their hands free, but their arms tied to their sides, so that each of them was able to carry a crucifix; they held these close to their eyes. The sleeves of their gowns were very wide, so that one saw their arms, which were covered by sleeved shifts fastened at the wrists, as is the custom in this country.

Donna Lucrezia, whose heart was less stout, wept almost continuously; the young Beatrice, on the other hand, shewed great courage; and, turning to gaze at each of the churches by which the procession passed, would fall on her knees for a moment and say in a firm voice: *"Adoramus Te, Christe!"*

Meanwhile, poor Giacomo Cenci was being tortured upon the cart, and shewed great constancy.

The procession had difficulty in crossing the lower end

of the Piazza del Ponte Sant' Angelo, so great was the number of carriages and the crowd of people. The women were taken straight to the chapel which had been made ready, and there Giacomo Cenci was afterwards brought.

Young Bernardo, wrapped in his striped cloak, was taken straight to the scaffold; whereupon everyone thought that he was going to be put to death, and had not been pardoned. The poor boy was so frightened that he fell in a faint as soon as he had stepped on to the scaffold. He was revived with cold water and made to sit opposite the *mannaja*.

The executioner went to fetch Donna Lucrezia Petroni; her hands were tied behind her back, the veil no longer covered her shoulders. She appeared on the piazza accompanied by the banner, her head wrapped in the veil of black taffeta; there she made an act of reconciliation to God and kissed the Sacred Wounds. She was told to leave her slippers on the pavement; as she was very stout, she had some difficulty in climbing the scaffold. When she was on the scaffold and the black taffeta veil was taken from her, she was greatly ashamed to be seen with bare shoulders and bosom; she examined herself, then the *mannaja,* and, as a sign of resignation, raised her shoulders slightly; tears came to her eyes, she said: "O my God! . . . And you, my brethren, pray for my soul."

Not knowing what was expected of her, she asked Alessandro, the chief headsman, what she ought to do. He told her to place herself astride the plank of the block. But this position seemed to her offensive to modesty, and she took a long time to assume it. (The details which follow are endurable by the Italian public, which likes to know everything with the utmost exactitude; let it suffice the French reader to know that this poor woman's modesty led to her injuring her bosom; the executioner shewed her head to the people and then wrapped it in the black taffeta veil.)

While the *mannaja* was being put in order for the girl, a scaffold loaded with spectators fell, and many people were killed. They thus appeared in God's presence before Beatrice.

When Beatrice saw the banner returning to the chapel to fetch her, she asked boldly:

"Is my lady mother really dead?"

They replied that it was so; she fell on her knees before the crucifix and prayed fervently for her stepmother's soul. Then she spoke aloud and at great length to the crucifix.

"Lord, Thou hast come back for me, and I will follow Thee with a willing heart, despairing not of Thy mercy for my great sin," etc.

She then repeated several Psalms and prayers, all in praise of God. When at length the executioner appeared before her with a cord, she said:

"Bind this body which is to be punished, and unbind this soul which is to win immortality and an eternal glory."

Then she rose, said her prayer, left her slippers at the foot of the steps and, having mounted the scaffold, stepped nimbly across the plank, placed her neck beneath the *mannaja,* and made all the arrangements perfectly herself, so as to avoid being touched by the executioner. By the swiftness of her movements she prevented the crowd, at the moment when the taffeta veil was taken from her, from seeing her shoulders and bosom. The blow was a long time in falling, as an interruption occurred. During this time she called in a loud voice upon Jesus Christ and the Most Holy Virgin.[1] Her body sprang with an impulsive

---

[1] A contemporary writer states that Clement VIII was extremely uneasy as to the salvation of Beatrice's soul; as he knew that she had been unjustly sentenced, he feared an impatient revulsion. The moment she had placed her head upon the *mannaja,* the fortress of Sant' Angelo, from which the *mannaja* was plainly visible, fired a gun. The Pope, who

movement at the fatal instant. Poor Bernardo Cenci, who had remained seated on the scaffold, fell once again in a faint, and it took his *confortatori* a good half hour and more to revive him. Then there appeared upon the scaffold Giacomo Cenci; but here again we must pass over details that are too harrowing. Giacomo Cenci was "broken" (*mazzolato*).

Immediately, Bernardo was taken back to prison; he was in a high fever and was bled.

As for the poor women, each of them was placed in her coffin and laid down a few feet away from the scaffold, near the statue of Saint Paul, which is the first on the right-hand side on the Ponte Sant' Angelo. Round each coffin burned four candles of white wax.

Later, with all that remained of Giacomo Cenci, they were conveyed to the palace of the Florentine Consul. At a quarter past nine in the evening,[1] the body of the girl, dressed in her own clothes and covered with a profusion of flowers, was carried to San Pietro in Montorio. She was exquisitely beautiful; looking at her, one would have said that she was asleep. She was buried in front of the high altar, and of Raphael's *Transfiguration*. She was escorted by fifty great candles, lighted, and by all the Franciscans in Rome.

Lucrezia Petroni was carried, at ten o'clock at night, to the Church of San Giorgio. During the course of this tragedy, the crowd was beyond number; as far as the eye

was engaged in prayer at Monte Cavallo, awaiting this signal, at once gave the girl the Papal major absolution *in articulo mortis*. This accounts for the delay in carrying out the sentence, of which the chronicler speaks.

[1] This is the hour set apart, in Rome, for the obsequies of Princes. The funeral of a citizen starts at sunset; the lesser nobility are carried to church at the first hour of night, Cardinals and Princes at half-past two of the night, which, on the 11th of September, corresponds to a quarter to ten.

could reach, one saw the streets packed with carriages and people, scaffoldings, windows and roofs covered with curious spectators. The sun's heat was so intense that day that many people lost consciousness. Any number of them took fever; and when the whole affair was at an end, at the nineteenth hour (a quarter to two), and the crowd dispersed, many people were suffocated, others trampled down by the horses. The number of deaths was considerable.

Donna Lucrezia Petroni was of middle height, or a little shorter, and, although fifty years old, was still a handsome woman. She had very fine features, a small nose, dark eyes, the skin of her face quite white with a fine complexion; her hair, which was not abundant, was chestnut.

Beatrice Cenci, who must inspire undying regret, was just sixteen; she was of short stature; her figure was charmingly rounded, and there were dimples in the centre of her cheeks, so that, lying dead and garlanded with flowers, she appeared to be asleep and even smiling, as she had so often lain when she was alive. Her mouth was small, her hair golden, and naturally curling. As she went to the scaffold these fair ringlets fell over her eyes, which gave her a certain charm and inspired pity.

Giacomo Cenci was of short stature, stout, with a pale face and black beard; he was about twenty-six years old when he died.

Bernardo Cenci closely resembled his sister, and as he wore his hair long like hers, many people, when he appeared on the scaffold, mistook him for her.

The heat of the sun had been so intense that a number of the spectators of this tragedy died during the night, and among them Ubaldino Ubaldini, a young man of rare beauty who had until then been in perfect health. He was brother to Signor Renzi, so well known in Rome.

Thus the shades of the Cenci left this world numerously escorted.

Yesterday, which was Tuesday the 14th of September, 1599, the penitents of San Marcello, on the occasion of the Feast of the Holy Cross, made use of their privilege to deliver from prison Don Bernardo Cenci, who has bound himself to pay within a year four hundred thousand francs to the Santissima Trinità del Ponte Sisto.

Added by another hand.

It is from him that the Francesco and Bernardo Cenci, now alive, descend.

The famous Farinacci, who, by his persistence, saved young Cenci's life, afterwards published his pleadings. He gives only an extract from pleading no. 66, which he declaimed before Clement VIII on behalf of the Cenci. This pleading, in the Latin tongue, would occupy fully six pages, and I cannot insert it here; this I regret, as it portrays the mental attitude of 1599; it seems to me eminently reasonable. Many years after 1599, Farinacci, when sending his pleadings to the press, added a note to this speech in defence of the Cenci: *Omnes fuerunt ultimo supplicio effecti, excepto Bernardo qui ad triremes cum bonorum confiscatione condemnatus fuit, ac etiam ad interessendum aliorum morti prout interfuit.* The end of this Latin note is touching, but I expect the reader is tired of so long a story.

THE ABBESS OF
CASTRO

THE ABBESS OF CASTRO

I

WE have so often been shewn in melodrama the
Italian brigands of the sixteenth century, and
so many people have spoken of them without
any real knowledge, that we have come to hold the most er-
roneous ideas of what they were like. Speaking generally,
one may say that these brigands were the *Opposition* to the
vile governments which, in Italy, took the place of the
mediaeval Republics. The new tyrant was, as a rule, the
wealthiest citizen of the defunct Republic, and, to win over
the populace, would adorn the town with splendid churches
and fine pictures. Such were the Polentini of Ravenna, the
Manfredi of Faenza, the Riario of Imola, the Cani of
Verona, the Bentivoglio of Bologna, the Visconti of Milan,
and lastly, the least bellicose and most hypocritical of all,
the Medici of Florence. Among the historians of these little
States none has dared to relate the countless poisonings
and assassinations ordered by the fear that used to torment
these petty tyrants; these grave historians were in their
pay. When you consider that each of these tyrants was
personally acquainted with each of the Republicans by
whom he knew himself to be execrated (the Tuscan Grand
Duke Cosimo, for instance, knew Strozzi), and that several
of these tyrants died by the hand of the assassin, you will
understand the profound hatreds, the eternal distrust which
gave so much spirit and courage to the Italians of the six-
teenth century, and such genius to their artists. You will
see these profound passions preventing the birth of that

really rather absurd prejudice which was called *honour* in the days of Madame de Sévigné, and consists first and foremost in sacrificing one's life to serve the master whose subject one is by birth, and to please the ladies. In the sixteenth century, a man's activity and his real worth could not be displayed in France, nor win admiration, except by bravery on the field of battle or in duels; and, as women love bravery, and above all daring, they became the supreme judges of a man's worth. Then was born the *spirit of gallantry*, which led to the destruction, one after another, of all the passions, including love, in the interests of that cruel tyrant whom we all obey: namely, vanity. Kings protected vanity, and with good reason, hence the power of the riband.

In Italy, a man distinguished himself by *all forms* of merit, by famous strokes with the sword as by discoveries in ancient manuscripts: take Petrarch, the idol of his time; and a woman of the sixteenth century loved a man who was learned in Greek as well as, if not more than she would have loved a man famous for his martial valour. Then one saw passions, and not the habit of gallantry. That is the great difference between Italy and France, that is why Italy has given birth to a Raphael, a Giorgione, a Titian, a Correggio, while France produced all those gallant captains of the sixteenth century, so entirely forgotten to-day, albeit each of them had killed so vast a number of enemies.

I ask pardon for these homely truths. However it be, the atrocious and *necessary* acts of vengeance of the petty Italian tyrants of the middle ages won over the hearts of their peoples to the brigands. The brigands were hated when they stole horses, corn, money, in a word everything that was necessary to support life; but, in their heart of hearts, the people were for them, and the village girls preferred to all the rest the boy who once in his life had been obliged *andare alla macchia,* that is to say to flee to

the woods and take refuge among the brigands, in conse-
quence of some over-rash action.

And even in our own day everyone dreads, unquestion-
ably, an encounter with brigands; but when they are caught
and punished everyone is sorry for them. The fact is that
this people, so shrewd, so cynical, which laughs at all the
publications issued under the official censure of its masters,
finds its favourite reading in little poems which narrate
with ardour the lives of the most renowned brigands. The
heroic element that it finds in these stories thrills the
artistic vein that still survives in the lower orders, and
besides, they are so weary of the official praise given to
certain people, that everything of this sort which is not
official goes straight to the heart. It must be explained
that the lower classes in Italy suffer from certain things
which the traveller would never observe, were he to live
ten years in the country. For instance, fifteen years ago,
before governments in their wisdom had suppressed the
brigands,[1] it was not uncommon to see certain of their
exploits punish the iniquities of the *Governors* of small
towns. These Governors, absolute magistrates whose emolu-
ments do not amount to more than twenty scudi monthly,
are naturally at the disposal of the most important family
of the place, which by this simple enough method op-
presses its enemies. If the brigands did not always suc-
ceed in punishing these despotic little Governors, they
did at least make fools of them, and defy their authority,
which is no small matter in the eyes of this quick-witted
race. A satirical sonnet consoles them for all their mis-

[1] Gasparone, the last of the brigands, made terms with the
Government in 1826; he was confined in the citadel of Civita-
Vecchia with thirty-two of his men. It was the want of water
on the heights of the Apennines, where he had taken refuge, that
obliged him to make terms. He was a man of spirit, with a face
that is not easily forgotten.

fortunes, and never do they forget an injury. That is another fundamental difference between the Italian and the Frenchman.

In the sixteenth century, had the Governor of a township sentenced to death a poor inhabitant who had incurred the hatred of the leading family, one often found brigands attacking the prison in an attempt to set free the victim; on the other hand the powerful family, having no great faith in the nine or ten soldiers of the government who were set to guard the prison, would raise at its own expense a troop of temporary soldiers. These latter, who were known as *bravi,* would install themselves in the neighbourhood of the prison, and make it their business to escort to the place of execution the poor devil whose death had been bought. If the powerful family included a young man, he would place himself at the head of these improvised soldiers.

This state of civilisation makes morality groan, I admit; in our day we have the duel, dulness, and judges are not bought and sold; but these sixteenth century customs were marvellously well adapted to create men worthy of the name.

Many historians, praised even to-day in the hack literature of the academies, have sought to conceal this state of affairs, which, about the year 1550, was forming such great characters. At the time, their prudent falsehoods were rewarded with all the honours which the Medici of Florence, the Este of Ferrara, the Viceroys of Naples and so forth had at their disposal. One poor historian, named Giannone, did seek to raise a corner of the veil, but as he ventured only to tell a very small part of the truth, and even then only by using ambiguous and obscure expressions, he made himself extremely tedious, which did not prevent him from dying in prison at the age of eighty-two, on March 7th, 1758.

The first thing to be done, then, if one wishes to learn the history of Italy, is on no account to read the authors generally commended; nowhere has the value of a lie been better appreciated, nowhere has lying been better rewarded.[1]

The earliest histories to be written in Italy, after the great wave of barbarism in the ninth century, make mention already of the brigands, and speak of them as though they had existed from time immemorial. (See Muratori's collection.) When, unfortunately for the general welfare, for justice, for good government, but fortunately for the arts, the mediaeval Republics were overthrown, the most energetic among the Republicans, those who loved freedom more than the majority of their fellow-citizens, took refuge in the forests. Naturally a populace harassed by the Baglioni, the Malatesta, the Bentivoglio, the Medici, etc., loved and respected their enemies. The cruelties of the petty tyrants who succeeded the first usurpers, the cruelties, for instance, of Cosimo, the first Duke of Florence, who had the Republicans who had fled to Venice, and even to Paris, slain, furnished recruits to these brigands. To speak only of the times in which our heroine lived, about the year 1550, Alfonso Piccolomini, Duca di Monte Mariano, and Marco Sciarra led with success armed bands which, in the neighbourhood of Albano, used to brave the Pope's soldiers, who at that time were very brave indeed. The line of operations of these famous chiefs, whom the populace still admire, extended from

[1] Paolo Giovio, Bishop of Como, Aretino, and a hundred others less amusing, whom the dulness that they diffuse has saved from disrepute, Robertson, Roscoe are full of lies. Guicciardini sold himself to Cosimo I, who treated him with contempt. In our time, Coletta and Pignotti have told the truth, the latter with the constant fear of being disgraced, although he refused to allow his work to be printed until after his death.

the Po and the marshes of Ravenna as far as the woods that then covered Vesuvius. The forest of la Faggiola, rendered so famous by their exploits, and situated five leagues from Rome, on the way to Naples, was the head-quarters of Sciarra, who, during the Pontificate of Gregory XIII, had often several thousands of men under his command. The detailed history of this illustrious brigand would appear incredible to the present generation, for the reason that no one would ever be able to understand the motives of his actions. He was not defeated until 1592. When he saw that his affairs were in a desperate state, he made terms with the Venetian Republic, and transferred himself to its service, with the most devoted, or most criminal (as you please) of his men. At the request of the Roman Government, Venice, which had signed a treaty with Sciarra, had him put to death, and sent his brave soldiers to defend the Isle of Candia against the Turks. But Venice in her wisdom knew well that a deadly plague was raging in Candia, and in a few days the five hundred soldiers whom Sciarra had brought to the service of the Republic were reduced to sixty-seven.

This forest of la Faggiola, whose giant trees screen an extinct volcano, was the final scene of the exploits of Marco Sciarra. Every traveller will tell you that it is the most impressive spot in that marvellous Roman Campagna, whose sombre aspect appears made for tragedy. It crowns with its dusky verdure the summit of Monte Albano.

It is to a volcanic eruption centuries earlier than the foundation of Rome that we owe this splendid mountain. At an epoch before any of the histories, it rose in the midst of the vast plain which at one time extended from the Apennines to the sea. Monte Cavi, which rises surrounded by the dusky shade of la Faggiola, is its culminating point: it is visible from all sides, from Terracina and

Ostia as well as from Rome and Tivoli, and it is the mountain of Albano, covered now with palaces, which closes to the south that Roman horizon so familiar to travellers. A convent of Blackfriars has taken the place, on the summit of Monte Cavi, of the temple of Jupiter Feretrius, where the Latin peoples came to sacrifice in common and to confirm the bonds of a sort of religious federation. Protected by the shade of magnificent chestnuts, the traveller arrives after some hours at the enormous blocks which mark the ruins of the temple of Jupiter; but beneath this dark shade, so delicious in that climate, even to-day, the traveller peers anxiously into the depths of the forest; he is afraid of brigands. On reaching the summit of Monte Cavi, we light a fire in the ruins of the temple, to prepare our meal. From this point, which commands the whole of the Roman Campagna, we perceive, to the west of us, the sea, which seems to be within a stone's throw, although three or four leagues away; we can distinguish the smallest vessels; with the least powerful glass, we can count the people who are journeying to Naples on board the steamer. To all the other points of the compass, the view extends over a magnificent plain, which is bounded on the east by the Apennines above Palestrina, and to the north by Saint Peter's and the other great buildings of Rome. Monte Cavi being of no great height, the eye can make out the minutest details of this sublime landscape, which might well dispense with any historical association, and yet every clump of trees, every fragment of ruined wall, catching the eye in the plain or on the slopes of the mountain, recalls one of those battles, so admirable for their patriotism and their valour, which Livy has put on record.

And we to-day can still follow, on our way to the enormous blocks, the remains of the temple of Jupiter Feretrius, which serve as a wall to the garden of the

Blackfriars, the *triumphal road* travelled long ago by the first Kings of Rome. It is paved with stones cut with great regularity; and, in the middle of the forest of la Faggiola, we come upon long sections of it.

On the lip of the crater which, filled now with clear water, has become the charming lake of Albano, five or six miles in circumference, so deeply embedded in its socket of lava, stood Alba, the mother of Rome, which Roman policy destroyed in the days of the first kings. Its ruins, however, still exist. Some centuries later, a quarter of a league from Alba, on the slope of the mountain that faces the sea, arose Albano, the modern city; but it is divided from the lake by a screen of rocks which hide the lake from the city and the city from the lake. When one sees it from the plain, its white buildings stand out against the dark, profound verdure of the forest so dear to the brigands and so often made famous, which crowns the volcanic mountain on every side.

Albano, which numbers to-day five or six thousand inhabitants, had not three thousand in 1540, when there flourished, in the highest rank of the nobility, the powerful family of Campireali, whose misfortunes we are about to relate.

I translate this story from two bulky manuscripts, one Roman, the other Florentine. At great risk to myself, I have ventured to reproduce their style, which is more or less that of our old legends. So fine and restrained a style as is fashionable at the present day would, I feel, have been too little in keeping with the events recorded, and less still with the reflexions of the writers. They wrote about the year 1598. I crave the reader's indulgence as well for them as for myself.

II

"HAVING committed to writing so many tragic histories," says the author of the Florentine manuscript, "I shall conclude with that one which, among them all, it most pains me to relate. I am going to speak of that famous Abbess of the Convent of the Visitation at Castro, Elena de' Campireali, whose trial and death caused so great a stir in the high society of Rome and of Italy. As far back as 1555, brigands reigned in the neighbourhood of Rome, the magistrates were sold to the powerful families. In the year 1572, which was that of the trial, Gregory XIII, Buoncompagni, ascended the Throne of Saint Peter. This holy pontiff combined all the apostolic virtues but has been blamed for a certain weakness in his civil government: he was unable either to select honest judges or to suppress the brigands; he burdened his soul with crimes which he could not punish. He felt that, in inflicting the death penalty, he was taking upon himself a terrible responsibility. The result of this attitude was to people with an almost innumerable host of brigands the roads that lead to the eternal city. To travel with any security, one had to be a friend of the brigands. The forest of la Faggiola, lying astride of the road that runs to Naples by Albano, had long been the headquarters of a government unfriendly to that of His Holiness, and on several occasions Rome was obliged to treat, as one power with another, with Marco Sciarra, one of the kings of the forest. What gave these brigands their strength was that they had endeared themselves to their peasant neighbours.

[53]

"This charming town of Albano, so close to the brigand headquarters, witnessed the birth, in 1542, of Elena de' Campireali. Her father was reckoned the wealthiest patrician of the district, and in this capacity had married Vittoria Carafa, who owned a large estate in the Kingdom of Naples. I could name several old men still living who knew both Vittoria Carafa and her daughter quite well. Vittoria was a model of prudence and sense; but despite all her cleverness she could not avert the ruin of her family. And this is curious: the terrible misfortunes which are to form the melancholy subject of my story cannot, it seems to me, be ascribed especially to any of the actors whom I am going to present to the reader: I see people who are unfortunate, but truly I cannot find any that are to be blamed. The extreme beauty and tender heart of the young Elena were two great perils for her, and form an excuse for Giulio Branciforte, her lover, just as the absolute want of sense of Monsignor Cittadini, Bishop of Castro, may excuse him also up to a certain point. He had owed his rapid advancement in the scale of ecclesiastical dignities to the honesty of his conduct, and above all to the most noble bearing and most regularly handsome features that one could hope to meet. I find it written of him that one could not set eyes on him without loving him.

"As I do not wish to flatter anyone, I shall make no attempt to conceal the fact that a holy friar of the Convent of Monte Cavi, who had often been surprised, in his cell, floating at a height of several feet from the ground, like Saint Paul, when nothing but divine grace could maintain him in that extraordinary posture,[1] had prophesied

---

[1] Even to-day, this singular position is regarded by the populace of the Roman Campagna as a sure sign of sanctity. About the year 1826, a monk of Albano was seen many times raised from the ground by divine grace. Many miracles were ascribed

to Signor de' Campireali that his family would be extinguished with him, and that he would have but two children, each of whom was to perish by a violent death. It was on account of this prophecy that he could find no one to marry in the district, and went to seek his fortune at Naples, where he was lucky enough to find great possessions and a wife capable, by her intelligence, of averting his evil destiny, had such a thing been possible. This Signor de' Campireali was considered a most honourable man, and dispensed charity lavishly; but he lacked spirit, which meant that gradually he withdrew from the annual visit to Rome, and ended by passing almost the whole year in his palazzo at Albano. He devoted himself to the cultivation of his estates, situated in that rich plain which extends from the city to the sea. On the advice of his wife, he caused the most splendid education to be given to his son Fabio, a young man extremely proud of his birth, and his daughter Elena, who was a marvel of beauty, as may be seen to this day from her portrait, which is preserved in the Farnese collection. Since I began to write her history I have gone to the palazzo Farnese to consider the mortal envelope which heaven had bestowed upon this woman, whose grim destiny caused so much stir in her own time, and even now still finds a place in human memory. The shape of the head is an elongated oval, the brow is very large, the hair of a dark gold. Her general air is on the whole one of gaiety; she had large eyes with a profound expression, and chestnut eyebrows that formed a perfectly traced arch. The lips are very thin, and you would say that the lines of her mouth had been drawn by the famous painter Correggio. Viewed

to him; people came from a radius of twenty leagues to receive his blessing; women, belonging to the highest ranks of society, had seen him floating in his cell three feet from the ground. Suddenly he vanished.

amid the portraits which hang on either side of hers in the Farnese gallery, she has the air of a queen. It is very seldom that an air of gaiety is found in combination with majesty.

"Having spent eight whole years as a boarder in the Convent of the Visitation in the town of Castro, now destroyed, to which, in those days, the majority of the Roman princes sent their daughters, Elena returned to her home, but did not leave the convent without first making an oblation of a splendid chalice to the high altar of the church. No sooner had she returned to Albano than her father summoned from Rome, at a considerable salary, the celebrated poet Cecchino, then a man of great age; he enriched Elena's mind with the finest passages of the divine Virgil, and of Petrarch, Ariosto and Dante, his famous disciples."

Here the translator is obliged to omit a long dissertation on the varying degrees of fame which the sixteenth century assigned to these great poets. It would appear that Elena knew Latin. The poetry that she was made to learn spoke of love, and of a love that would seem to us highly ridiculous, were we to come across it in 1839; I mean the passionate love that feeds on great sacrifices, that can exist only when wrapped in mystery, and borders always on the most dreadful calamities.

Such was the love that was inspired in Elena, then barely seventeen, by Giulio Branciforte. He was one of her neighbours, and very poor; he lived in a wretched house built on the side of the mountain, a quarter of a league from the town, amid the ruins of Alba, and on the edge of the precipice of one hundred and fifty feet, screened with foliage, which surrounds the lake. This house, which stood within the sombre and splendid shade of the forest of la Faggiola, was afterwards demolished, when the convent of Palazzuola was built. The poor young man had no advantages beyond his lively and light-hearted manner and the unfeigned indifference with which he endured his misfortunes. The most that could be said in his favour was that his face was expressive without being handsome. But he was understood to have fought gallantly under the command of Prince Colonna, and among his *bravi*, in two or three highly dangerous enterprises. Despite his poverty, despite his want of good looks, he possessed nevertheless, in the eyes of all the young women of Albano, the heart that it would have been most gratifying to win. Well received everywhere, Giulio Branciforte had made none but the easiest conquests, until the moment when Elena returned from the convent of Castro. "When, shortly afterwards, the great poet Cecchino moved from Rome to the palazzo Campireali, to teach the girl literature, Giulio, who knew him, sent him a set of Latin verses on the good fortune that had befallen him in his old age, in seeing so fine a pair of eyes fastened upon his own, and so pure a heart become perfectly happy when he deigned to bestow his approval upon its thoughts. The jealousy and disgust of the girls to whom Giulio had been paying attention before Elena's return soon rendered vain every precaution that he might take to conceal a dawning passion, and I must confess that this affair between a young man of two and twenty and a girl of seventeen was carried on in a fashion of which prudence could not approve. Three months had not gone by before Signor de' Campireali observed that Giulio Branciforte was in the habit of passing unduly often beneath the windows of his palazzo (which is still to be seen about half way along the high road that leads up to the lake)."

Freedom of speech and rudeness, natural consequences of the liberty which Republics tolerate, and the habit of giving way to passions not yet subdued by the manners of a monarchy appear unconcealed in the first steps taken by Signor de' Campireali. On the very day on which he had taken offence at the frequent appearance of young Branciforte, he addressed him in these terms:

"How is it you dare loiter about like this all day in front of my house, and have the impertinence to stare up at my daughter's windows, you who have not even a coat to your back? Were I not afraid that such an action might be misinterpreted by my neighbours, I should give you three gold sequins, and you would go to Rome and buy yourself a more decent jacket. At any rate my eyes and my daughter's would not be offended any more by the sight of your rags."

Elena's father no doubt exaggerated: young Branciforte's clothes were by no means rags; they were made of the plainest materials; but, although spotlessly clean and often brushed, it must be admitted that their appearance betokened long wear. Giulio was so cut to the heart by Signor Campireali's reproaches that he ceased to appear by day outside his house.

As we have said, the two lines of arches, remains of an ancient aqueduct, which formed the main walls of the house built by Branciforte's father and left by him to his son, were no more than five or six hundred yards from Albano. In coming down from this higher ground to the modern city, Giulio was obliged to pass by the palazzo Campireali. Elena soon remarked the absence of the singular young man who, her friends told her, had abandoned all other society in order to consecrate himself wholly to the pleasure which he appeared to find in gazing at her.

One summer evening, towards midnight, Elena's window stood open, the girl herself was enjoying the sea breeze which makes itself felt quite distinctly on the hillside of Albano, albeit the town is divided from the sea by a plain three leagues in width. The night was dark, the silence profound; one could have heard a leaf fall to the ground. Elena, leaning upon her window sill, may have been thinking of Giulio, when she caught sight of something like the soundless wing of a nocturnal bird which passed gently to and fro close to her window. She drew back in alarm. It never occurred to her that this object might be being held up by some passer-by: the second storey of the palazzo, from which her window looked, was more than fifty feet from the ground. Suddenly she thought she identified a bunch of flowers in this strange article which amid a profound silence kept passing to and fro outside the window on the sill of which she was leaning; her heart beat violently. These flowers appeared to her to be fastened to the extremity of two or three of those *canne,* a large kind of reed not unlike the bamboo, which grow in the Roman Campagna, and send up shoots to a height of twenty or thirty feet. The flexibility of the reeds and the strength of the breeze made it difficult for Giulio to keep his nosegay exactly opposite the window from which he supposed that Elena might be looking out, and besides, the night was so dark that from the street one could make out nothing at that height. Standing motionless inside her window, Elena was deeply stirred. To take these flowers, would not that be an admission? Not that she experienced any of the feelings to which an adventure of this sort would give rise, in our day, in a girl of the best society prepared for life by a thorough education. As her father and her brother Fabio were in the house, her first thought was that the least sound would be followed by a shot from an arquebus aimed at Giulio; she was moved to pity by the risk which that poor young man was running. Her second thought was that, although she as yet knew him very slightly, he was nevertheless the person she loved best in the world after her own family. At length, after hesitating for some minutes, she took the nosegay, and, as she touched the flowers in the intense darkness, could feel that a note was tied to the stem of one of them; she ran to the great staircase to read this note by the light of the lamp that burned before the image of the Madonna. "How rash!" she said to herself when the opening lines had made her blush with joy; "If anyone sees me, I am lost, and my family will persecute that poor young man for ever." She returned to her room and lighted the lamp. This was an exquisite moment for Giulio, who, ashamed of his action and as though to hide himself even in the pitch darkness, had flattened himself against the enormous trunk of one of those weirdly shaped evergreen oaks which are still to be seen opposite the palazzo Campireali.

In his letter Giulio related with the most perfect simplicity the crushing reprimand that had been addressed to him by Elena's father. "I am poor, it is true," he went on, "and you would find it hard to imagine the whole extent of my poverty. I have only my house which you may have observed beneath the ruins of the Alban aqueduct; round the house is a garden which I cultivate myself, and live upon its produce. I also possess a vineyard which is leased at thirty scudi a year. I do not know, really, why I love you; certainly I cannot suggest that you should come and share my poverty. And yet, if you do not love me, life has no further value for me; it is useless to tell you that I would give it a thousand times over for you. And yet, before your return from the convent, that life was by no means wretched; on the contrary, it was filled with the most dazzling dreams. So that I can say that the sight of happiness has made me unhappy. To be sure, no one in the world would then have dared to say the things to me with which your father lashed me; my dagger would have done him prompt justice. Then, with my courage and my weapons, I reckoned myself a match for anyone; I

wanted nothing. Now it is all altered: I have known fear.
I have written too much; perhaps you despise me. If,
on the other hand, you have any pity for me, in spite of
the poor clothes that cover me, you will observe that every
night, when twelve strikes from the Capuchin convent at
the top of the hill, I am hiding beneath the great oak,
opposite the window at which I never cease to gaze, be-
cause I suppose it to be that of your room. If you do not
despise me as your father does, throw me down one of the
flowers from your nosegay, but take care that it is not
caught on one of the cornices, or on one of the balconies
of your palazzo."

This letter was read many times; gradually Elena's eyes
filled with tears; she tenderly examined this splendid nose-
gay, the flowers of which were tied together with a strong
silken cord. She tried to pull out a flower, but failed;
then she was seized with remorse. Among Roman girls,
to pull out a flower, to damage in any way a nosegay given
in love, means risking the death of that love. Fearing
lest Giulio might be growing impatient, she ran to her
window; but, on reaching it, suddenly reflected that she
was too easily visible, the lamp flooding the room with
light. Elena could not think what signal she might allow
herself to give; it seemed as though there were none that
did not say a great deal too much.

Covered with shame, she ran back into her room. But
time was flying; suddenly an idea occurred to her which
threw her into unspeakable confusion: Giulio would think
that, like her father, she despised his poverty! She saw
a little specimen of a precious marble lying on her table,
tied it in her handkerchief and threw the handkerchief
down to the foot of the oak opposite her window. She
then made a sign that he was to go; she heard Giulio obey
her; for, as he went away, he no longer sought to muffle
the sound of his step. When he had reached the summit

of the girdle of rocks which separates the lake from the last houses of Albano, she heard him singing words of love; she made him signals of farewell, this time less timid, then began to read his letter again.

The following evening, and every evening after this there were similar letters and assignations; but as everything is observed in an Italian village, and as Elena was by far the greatest heiress in the place, Signor de' Campireali was informed that every evening, after midnight, a light was seen in his daughter's room; and, what was far more extraordinary, the window was open, and indeed Elena stood there as though she were in no fear of *zanzare* (an extremely troublesome kind of midge, which greatly spoils the fine evenings in the Roman Campagna. Here I must once again crave the reader's indulgence. When one is trying to understand the ways of foreign countries, one must expect to find very grim ideas, very different from our own). Signor de' Campireali made ready his own arquebus and his son's. That evening, as the clock struck a quarter to twelve, he called Fabio, and the two stole out, making as little sound as possible, on to a great stone balcony which projected from the first floor of the palazzo immediately beneath Elena's window. The massive pillars of the stone balustrade gave them breast-high cover from the fire of any arquebus that might be aimed at them from without. Midnight struck; father and son could hear quite distinctly a slight sound from beneath the trees which bordered the street opposite their palazzo; but, and this filled them with surprise, no light appeared at Elena's window. This girl, so simple until then, and to all appearances a child, from the spontaneity of her movements, had changed in character since she had been in love. She knew that the slightest imprudence jeopardised her lover's life; if a gentleman of the importance of her father killed a poor man like Giulio Branciforte, he could clear himself by disappearing for three months, which he would spend at Naples; during that time, his friends in Rome would settle the matter, and all would be ended with the offer of a silver lamp costing some hundreds of scudi to the altar of the Madonna in fashion at the moment. That day, at luncheon, Elena had read on her father's features that he had some grave cause for anger, and, from the way in which he watched her when he thought that he was not observed, she concluded that she herself was largely responsible for this anger. She went at once and sprinkled a little dust on the stocks of the five splendid arquebuses which her father kept hanging by his bed. She covered also with a fine layer of dust his swords and daggers. All day she shewed a wild gaiety, running incessantly from top to bottom of the house; at every moment she went to the windows, quite determined to make Giulio a negative signal, should she be so fortunate as to catch sight of him. But there was no chance of that: the poor fellow had been so profoundly humiliated by the onslaught made on him by the rich Signor de' Campireali, that by day he never appeared in Albano; duty alone brought him there on Sundays to the parochial mass. Elena's mother, who adored her and could refuse her nothing, went out with her three times that day, but all in vain: Elena saw no sign of Giulio. She was in despair. What were her feelings when, on going towards nightfall to examine her father's weapons, she saw that two arquebuses had been loaded, and that almost all the swords and daggers had been handled. She was distracted from her mortal anxiety only by the extreme care she took to appear to suspect nothing. On retiring to bed at ten o'clock, she turned the key in the door of her room, which opened into her mother's ante-room, then remained glued to her window, leaning upon the sill in such a way as not to be visible from without. One may judge of the anxiety

with which she heard the hours strike: it was no longer
a question of the reproaches which she often heaped on
herself for the rapidity with which she had attached her-
self to Giulio, which might render her less worthy in his
eyes of love. This day did more to strengthen the young
man's position than six months of constancy and protesta-
tions. "What is the use of lying?" Elena said to herself.
"Do I not love him with all my heart and soul?"

At half past eleven she saw quite plainly her father and
brother ambush themselves on the great stone balcony be-
neath her window. A minute or two after midnight had
sounded from the Capuchin convent, she heard quite plainly
also the step of her lover, who stopped beneath the great
oak; she noticed with joy that her father and brother
seemed to have heard nothing: it required the anxiety of
love to distinguish so faint a sound.

"Now," she said to herself, "they are going to kill me,
but at all costs they must not intercept this evening's let-
ter, they would persecute my poor Giulio for ever." She
made the sign of the Cross, and, holding on with one hand
to the iron balcony of her window, leaned out, thrusting
herself as far forward as possible over the street. Not
a quarter of a minute had passed when the nosegay, fas-
tened as usual to a long cane, came brushing against her
arms. She seized the nosegay, but, as she wrenched it
vigorously from the cane to the end of which it was tied,
she caused the said cane to strike against the stone bal-
cony. At once two arquebus shots rang out, followed by
complete silence. Her brother Fabio, not knowing, in the
darkness, whether what was tapping violently against the
balcony might not be a cord with the help of which Giulio
was climbing down from his sister's room, had fired at her
balcony; next day she found the mark of the bullet, which
had flattened itself against the iron. Signor de' Campireali
had fired into the street, beneath the stone balcony, for

Giulio had made some noise in catching the cane as it fell. Giulio, for his part, hearing a noise above his head, had guessed what would follow, and had taken cover beneath the projection of the balcony.

Fabio quickly reloaded his arquebus, and, heedless of anything that his father might say, ran to the garden of the house, quietly opened a little door which gave on one of the adjoining streets and stole out on tiptoe to see for himself who the people were that were walking beneath the balcony of the palazzo. At that moment Giulio who, this evening, was well escorted, was within twenty paces of him, flattened against a tree. Elena, leaning from her balcony and trembling for her lover, at once began a conversation at the top of her voice with her brother, whom she could hear moving in the street; she asked him if he had killed the robbers.

"Do not imagine that I am taken in by your wicked tricks!" he called up to her from the street which he was exploring in every direction, "but prepare your tears, I am going to kill the insolent wretch who dares to approach your window."

No sooner had these words been uttered than Elena heard her mother knock at the door of her room.

She made haste to open it, saying that she could not conceive how the door had come to be locked.

"No make-believe with me, my dear angel," her mother told her; "your father is furious, and will perhaps kill you: come and lie down with me in my bed; and, if you have a letter, give it to me, I will hide it."

Elena said to her:

"Here is the nosegay; the letter is hidden among the flowers."

Scarcely were mother and daughter in bed, when Signor de' Campireali entered his wife's room; he came from her oratory, to which he had paid a visit, overturning everything in it. What impressed Elena was that her father, pale as a spectre, was acting in a slow, deliberate fashion, like a man who has entirely made up his mind. "I am as good as dead!" she said to herself.

"We rejoice that we have children," said her father as he passed by his wife's bed on his way to his daughter's room, trembling with rage, but affecting a perfect calm; "we rejoice that we have children, we ought rather to shed tears of blood when those children are girls. Great God! Is it indeed possible! Their loose conduct is capable of destroying the honour of a man who in sixty years has never given anyone the slightest hold over him."

So saying, he passed into his daughter's room.

"I am lost," Elena told her mother, "the letters are beneath the pedestal of the crucifix, beside the window."

At once the mother sprang out of bed and ran after her husband; she shouted out to him the most senseless things imaginable, to stimulate his anger; in this she was entirely successful. The old man became furious, he broke everything in his daughter's room; but the mother was able to remove the letters unobserved. An hour later, when Signor de' Campireali had returned to his own room next door to his wife's, and all was quiet in the house, the mother said to her daughter:

"Here are your letters, I have no wish to read them, you see what they might have cost us! If I were you, I would burn them. Good night, kiss me."

Elena returned to her own room, dissolved in tears; it seemed to her that, after these words from her mother, she no longer loved Giulio. Then she made ready to burn his letters; but, before destroying them, could not refrain from reading them again. She read them so carefully and so often that the sun was already high in the heavens when at length she determined to listen to the voice of reason.

On the following day, which was a Sunday, Elena
walked to the parish church with her mother; fortunately,
her father did not follow them. The first person on whom
her eyes fell in church was Giulio Branciforte. A glance
at him assured her that he was not injured. Her happi-
ness knew no bounds; the events of the night were a mil-
lion leagues away from her memory. She had prepared
five or six little notes scribbled on old scraps of paper
stained with a mixture of earth and water, such as might
naturally be found lying on the floor of a church; each of
these notes contained the same warning:

*"They have discovered all, except his name. He must
not appear again in the street; a certain person will come
here often."*

Elena let fall one of these scraps of paper; a glance
was sufficient to warn Giulio, who picked it up and van-
ished. On her return home, an hour later, she found on
the great staircase of the palazzo a fragment of paper
which attracted her attention by its exact resemblance to
those of which she had made use that morning. She took
possession of it, without even her mother's noticing any-
thing; and read:

*"In three days he will return from Rome, where he is
forced to go. There will be singing by daylight, on
market-days, above the din made by the peasants, about
ten o'clock."*

This departure for Rome seemed to Elena strange.
"Does it mean that he is afraid of my brother's arquebus?"
she asked herself sadly. Love pardons everything, except
a deliberate absence; that being the worst of tortures. In-
stead of passing in a delightful dream and being wholly
occupied in weighing the reasons that one has for loving
one's lover, life is then agitated by cruel doubts. "But,
after all, can I believe that he no longer loves me?" Elena
asked herself during the three long days of Branciforte's

absence. Suddenly her grief gave way to a wild joy: on the third day, she saw him appear in the full light of noon, strolling in the street in front of her father's palazzo. He was wearing new, almost grand clothes. Never had the nobility of his bearing and the gay and courageous simplicity of his features shone to better advantage; never either, before that day, had there been so much talk in Albano of Giulio's poverty. It was the men, the young men especially, who repeated that cruel word; the women, and especially the girls, never wearied in their praises of his fine appearance.

Giulio spent the whole day walking about the town; he appeared to be making up for the months of seclusion to which his poverty had condemned him. As befits a man in love, Giulio was well armed beneath his new tunic. Apart from his dirk and dagger, he had put on his *giacco* (a sort of long waistcoat of chain mail, extremely uncomfortable to wear, but a cure, to these Italian hearts, for a sad malady, the piercing attacks of which were incessantly felt in that age, I mean the fear of being killed at the street corner by one of the enemies one knew oneself to have). On the day in question, Giulio hoped for a glimpse of Elena, and moreover felt some repugnance at the thought of being left to his own company in his lonely house: for the following reason. Ranuccio, an old soldier of his father, after having served with him in ten campaigns in the troops of various *condottieri,* and finally in those of Marco Sciarra, had followed his captain when the latter's wounds forced him to retire. Captain Branciforte had reasons for not living in Rome: he was exposed there to the risk of meeting the sons of men whom he had killed; even at Albano, he was by no means anxious to place himself entirely at the mercy of constituted authority. Instead of buying or leasing a house in the town, he preferred to build one so situated that its occupant could see visit-

ors approaching a long way off. He found amid the ruins
of Alba an admirable site: one could, unobserved by indis-
creet visitors, slip away into the forest where ruled his
old friend and patron, Prince Fabrizio Colonna. Captain
Branciforte gave no thought to his son's future. When
he retired from the service, only fifty years old, but rid-
dled with wounds, he calculated that he had still some ten
years of life, and, having built his house, spent every year
a tenth part of what he had collected in the lootings of
towns and villages in which he had had the honour to take
part

He purchased the vineyard which brought in a rental
of thirty scudi to his son as a retort to the sneer of a
burgess of Albano, who had said to him, one day when he
was disputing hotly over the interests and honour of the
town, that it was evidently right and proper for so rich
a proprietor as himself to give advice to the *anziani* of
Albano. The captain bought the vineyard, and announced
that he would buy any number more: then, meeting his
critic in a solitary place, killed him with a pistol shot.

After eight years of this sort of life, the captain died;
his supporter Ranuccio adored Giulio; nevertheless, weary
of idleness, he took service once again in Prince Colonna's
band. He often came to see *his son Giulio,* for so he called
him, and, on the eve of a perilous assault which the Prince
was about to face in his fortress of la Petrella, he had
taken Giulio with him to fight. Finding him to be ex-
tremely brave:

"You must be mad," he told him, "and very easily sat-
isfied, to be living on the outskirts of Albano like the
humblest and poorest of its inhabitants, when with what
I have seen you do and your father's name you might be
a brilliant soldier of fortune among us, and, what is more,
make your fortune."

Giulio was tormented by these words; he knew the

[69]

Latin that had been taught him by a priest, but, as his father had always laughed at everything that the priest said apart from his Latin, he had absolutely no education. At the same time, despised for his poverty, isolated in his lonely house, he had acquired a certain commonsense which, by its boldness, would have astonished men of learning. For instance, before falling in love with Elena, and without knowing why, he loved war, but he felt a repugnance towards pillage, which, in the eyes of his father the captain and of Ranuccio, was like the short play intended to raise a laugh which follows the noble tragedy. Since he had been in love with Elena, this commonsense, the fruit of his solitary reflexions, had been torturing Giulio. So light-hearted before, he now dared not consult anyone as to his doubts, his heart was full of passion and misery. What would not Signor de' Campireali say if he knew him to be a soldier of fortune? This time, his reproaches would not be without foundation! Giulio had always reckoned upon the military profession, as a sure resource when he should have spent the price of the gold chains and other jewels which he had found in his father's strong-box. If Giulio had no scruple as to carrying off (he, so poor) the daughter of the rich Signor de' Campireali, it was because in those days fathers disposed of their property after their death as they pleased, and Signor de' Campireali might very well leave his daughter a thousand scudi as her entire fortune. Another problem kept Giulio's imagination closely occupied: first of all, in what city should he install young Elena after he had married her and carried her off from her father? Secondly, with what money was he to support her?

When Signor de' Campireali addressed to him that stinging reproach which he had felt so keenly, Giulio remained for two days a victim to the most violent rage and grief: he could not make up his mind either to kill the insolent old man, or to let him live. He passed whole nights in tears; at length he decided to consult Ranuccio, the one friend that he had in the world; but would that friend understand him? It was in vain that he sought for Ranuccio throughout the forest of la Faggiola, he was obliged to take the road to Naples, past Velletri, where Ranuccio was in command of an ambuscade: he was waiting there, with a large company, for Ruiz d'Avalos, a Spanish General, who was proceeding to Rome by land, forgetting that, not long since, before a large audience, he had spoken with contempt of the soldiers of fortune of the Colonna band. His chaplain reminded him most opportunely of this little circumstance, and Ruiz d'Avalos decided to charter a vessel and to approach Rome by sea.

As soon as Captain Ranuccio had heard Giulio's story:

"Describe to me exactly," he said to him, "the person of this Signor de' Campireali, that his imprudence may not cost the life of some worthy inhabitant of Albano. As soon as the business that is keeping us here is brought to an end one way or the other, you will take yourself off to Rome, where you will take care to shew yourself in the inns and other public places at all hours of the day; you must not let anyone suspect you, on account of your love for the daughter."

Giulio had great difficulty in calming the anger of his father's old comrade. He was obliged to lose his temper.

"Do you suppose that I am asking you for your sword?" he said finally. "Surely I have a sword, myself! I ask you for good advice."

Ranuccio ended every speech with these words:

"You are young, you have no wounds; the insult was public: a man who has lost his honour is despised, even by women."

Giulio told him that he desired time for further reflexion as to what his heart wished, and despite the protesta-

[71]

tions of Ranuccio, who was quite determined that he should take part in the attack upon the Spanish General's escort, where, he said, there would be honour to be won, not to mention the doubloons, Giulio returned alone to his little house. It was there that, the day before that on which Signor de' Campireali fired an arquebus at him, he had entertained Ranuccio and his corporal, who had come there from the neighbourhood of Velletri. Ranuccio employed force to open the little iron strong box in which his patron, Captain Branciforte, used to lock up the gold chains and other jewels which he did not choose to convert into cash immediately after an expedition. He found in it two scudi.

"I advise you to become a monk," he said to Giulio, "you have all the necessary virtues: love of poverty, here is a proof of it; humility, you allow yourself to be black-guarded in the public street by a rich townsman of Albano; you want only hypocrisy and gluttony."

Ranuccio insisted on putting fifty doubloons into the iron box.

"I give you my word," he said to Giulio, "that if within a month from to-day Signor de' Campireali is not buried with all the honours due to his nobility and wealth, my corporal here present will come with thirty men to pull down your little house and burn your wretched furniture. Captain Branciforte's son must not cut a poor figure in this world, on the strength of being in love."

When Signor de' Campireali and his son fired the two shots from their arquebuses, Ranuccio and the corporal had taken up their position beneath the stone balcony, and Giulio had the greatest possible difficulty in restraining them from killing Fabio, when that young man made an imprudent sally through the garden, as we have already related. The argument that calmed Ranuccio was as follows: it is not right to kill a young man who may grow

up and become of use in the world, while there exists an
aged sinner more guilty than he, and fit only to fill a grave.
The day after this adventure, Ranuccio disappeared into
the forest, and Giulio set out for Rome. The joy which
he felt in buying fine clothes with the doubloons which
Ranuccio had given him, was cruelly marred by an idea
quite extraordinary for that time, and one that foreboded
the exalted destiny that was in store for him: he kept
saying to himself: "Elena must be told who I am." Any
other man of his age and period would have thought only
of enjoying his love and carrying off Elena, without ask-
ing himself for a moment what was to become of her in
six months' time, any more than what opinion she would
form of himself.

On his return to Albano, and on the afternoon of the
day on which he displayed before the eyes of all the town
the fine clothes that he had brought back from Rome,
Giulio learned from old Scotti, his friend, that Fabio had
left the town on horseback, on a journey of three leagues
to a property which his father owned in the plain, by the
sea-coast. Later in the day, he saw Signor de' Cam-
pireali, accompanied by two priests, take the road leading
to the magnificent avenue of evergreen oaks that crowns
the edge of the crater in which the lake of Albano lies.
Ten minutes later, an old woman boldly made her way
into the palazzo de' Campireali, on the pretext of offering
some fine fruit for sale; the first person that she met was
the little maid Marietta, the confidential friend of her mis-
tress Elena, who blushed to the whites of her eyes on re-
ceiving a fine nosegay. The letter concealed in the nose-
gay was of a preposterous length: Giulio related all his
feelings since the night of the arquebus-shots; but, by a
very singular piece of modesty, did not venture to confess
what any other young man of his day would have been so
proud to make known, namely that he was the son of a

Captain famous for his adventures, and that he himself
had already given proof of his valour in more than one
combat. He felt that he could hear the reflexions which
these deeds would inspire in old Campireali. It must be
understood that in the sixteenth century the young women,
their outlook being more akin to republican commonsense,
esteemed a man far more highly for what he had done
himself than for the riches amassed by his fathers or for
their famous deeds. But it was principally the young
women of humble birth that entertained these ideas. Those
who belonged to the rich or noble class were afraid of the
brigands, and, as is natural, had a great regard for no-
bility and opulence. Giulio ended his letter with the
words: "I do not know whether the more becoming clothes
which I have brought back from Rome have made you
forget the cruel insult that a person whom you respect
addressed to me recently, with regard to my shabby ap-
pearance; I could have avenged myself, I ought to have
done so, my honour commanded it; I refrained in consid-
eration of the tears which my revenge would have brought
to a pair of eyes that I adore. This may prove to you, if,
unfortunately for me, you should still doubt it, that one
can be extremely poor and yet have noble feelings. Apart
from this, I have to reveal to you a terrible secret; I should
certainly find no difficulty in telling it to any other woman;
but somehow I shudder when I think of making it known
to you. It is capable of destroying, in an instant, the
love that you feel for me; no protestation on your part
would satisfy me. I wish to read in your eyes the effect
that this admission will produce. One of these days, at
nightfall, I shall see you in the garden that lies behind
the palazzo. That day, Fabio and your father will be
away from home; when I have made certain that, notwith-
standing their contempt for a poor and ill dressed young
man, they cannot deprive us of three quarters of an hour

or an hour of conversation, a man will appear beneath the windows of your palazzo, who will be shewing a tame fox to the village children. Later, when the Angelus rings, you will hear a shot fired from an arquebus in the distance; at that moment, go across to the wall of your garden, and, if you are not alone, sing. If all is silent, your slave will appear, trembling, at your feet, and will tell you things which will perhaps fill you with horror. Until that decisive day comes, a terrible day for me, I shall not take the risk again of offering you a nosegay at midnight; but about two o'clock in the morning I shall go by singing, and perhaps, watching from the great stone balcony, you will let fall a flower plucked by you in your garden. These may be the last signs of affection that you will give to the unhappy Giulio."

Three days after this, Elena's father and brother had gone on their horses to the property which they owned by the seashore; they were to start back shortly before sunset, so as to reach home about two o'clock in the morning. But, when the time came for them to take the road, not only their own two horses but every horse on the farm had disappeared. Greatly astonished by this audacious robbery, they hunted for their horses, which were not found until the following day in the forest of tall trees which lines the shore. The two Campireali, father and son, were obliged to return to Albano in a country cart drawn by oxen.

That evening, when Giulio was at Elena's feet, it was almost quite dark, and the poor girl was very glad of the darkness: she was appearing for the first time before this man whom she loved tenderly, who knew very well that she loved him, but to whom after all she had never yet spoken.

One thing that she noticed restored a little of her courage: Giulio was paler and trembled more than she. She saw him at her knees: "Truly, I am not in a fit state to speak," he said to her. There followed some moments, apparently of great happiness; they gazed at one another, but without the power to utter a single word, motionless as a group wrought in marble, but a group full of expression. Giulio was on his knees, holding one of Elena's hands; she, with bent head, was studying him attentively.

Giulio knew well that, following the advice of his friends, the young debauchees of Rome, he ought to have made some attempt; but the idea horrified him. He was aroused from this state of ecstasy and, perhaps, of the keenest happiness that love can give, by this thought: the time was passing rapidly, the Campireali were drawing near their palazzo. He realised that with so scrupulous a nature as his he could not find any lasting happiness so long as he had not made to his mistress that terrible admission which would have seemed to his Roman friends so dense a piece of stupidity.

"I have spoken to you of an admission which perhaps I ought not to make to you," he said at length to Elena.

Giulio turned very pale; he added with difficulty and as though his breath were failing:

"Perhaps I am going to see those feelings vanish, the hope of which constitutes my life. You think me poor; that is not all: *I am a brigand and the son of a brigand.*"

At these words Elena, a rich man's daughter filled with all the fears of her caste, felt that she was going to faint; she was afraid of falling to the ground. "What a grief that will be for poor Giulio!" she thought: "he will imagine that I despise him." He was at her knees. In order not to fall she leaned upon him, and a little later fell into his arms, apparently unconscious. As we see, in the sixteenth century they liked exactitude in love stories. This was because the mind did not criticise these stories, the imagination felt them, and the passion of the reader iden-

tified itself with that of their heroes. The two manuscripts
which we follow, and especially the one which presents
certain turns of speech peculiar to the Florentine dialect,
give in the fullest detail the history of all the meetings
that followed. Danger took away all sense of guilt from
the girl. Often the danger was extreme; but it did nought
but inflame these two hearts for which all the sensations
that arose from their love were those of happiness. Sev-
eral times Fabio and his father were on the point of sur-
prising them. They were furious, believing themselves
to be defied: common rumour informed them that Giulio
was Elena's lover, and yet they could see nothing. Fabio,
an impetuous young man and one proud of his birth, pro-
posed to his father to have Giulio killed.

"So long as he remains in this world," he said to him,
"my sister's life is a succession of the greatest dangers.
Who knows but that at any moment our honour may oblige
us to dip our hands in the blood of that obstinate girl?
She has come to such a pitch of boldness that she no longer
denies her love; you have seen her answer your reproaches
only with a gloomy silence; very well, that silence is
Giulio Branciforte's death sentence."

"Think of what his father was," replied Signor de' Cam-
pireali. "Certainly there is no difficulty in our going to
spend six months in Rome, and, during that time, this
Branciforte will disappear. But how do we know that his
father, who, with all his crimes, was brave and generous,
generous to the point of enriching many of his soldiers
and remaining a poor man himself, how do we know that
his father has not left friends behind him, either in the
band of the Duca di Monte Mariano or in the Colonna
band, which often occupies the woods of la Faggiola, half
a league from us? In that case, we are all massacred
without mercy, you, myself, and perhaps your unfortu-
nate mother as well."

These conversations between the father and son, often repeated, were kept no secret from Vittoria Carafa, Elena's mother, and plunged her in despair. The upshot of Fabio's discussions with his father was that it did not become their honour to stand peacefully by and allow a continuance of the rumours that ran rife in Albano. Since it was not prudent to secure the disappearance of this young Branciforte who, every day, appeared more insolent than ever, and in addition, dressed now in magnificent clothes, carried his self-importance to the point of speaking, in the public thoroughfares, either to Fabio or to Signor de' Campireali himself, one, or possibly both of the following courses must be adopted: the whole family must return to live in Rome, or Elena must be sent back to the Convent of the Visitation at Castro, where she would remain until a suitable husband had been found for her.

Never had Elena confessed her love to her mother; daughter and mother loved one another tenderly, they spent their whole time together, and yet never had a single word been uttered on this subject which interested them both almost equally. For the first time the almost exclusive subject of their thoughts was expressed in words when the mother gave her daughter to understand that there was a question of removing the household to Rome, and perhaps of sending her back to spend some years in the Convent at Castro.

This conversation was imprudent on the part of Vittoria Carafa, and can be excused only by the unreasoning affection that she felt for her daughter. Elena, desperately in love, wished to prove to her lover that she was not ashamed of his poverty, and that her confidence in his honour knew no bounds. "Who would believe it?" cries the Florentine writer; "after all these daring assignations, attended with the risk of a horrible death, given in the garden, and once or twice even in her own room, Elena was pure! Strong in her virtue, she proposed to her lover that she should leave the palazzo, about midnight, by the garden, and spend the rest of the night in his little house built amid the ruins of Alba, more than a quarter of a league away. They disguised themselves as Franciscan friars. Elena was of tall stature, and, thus attired, appeared a young novice of eighteen or twenty. What is incredible, and shews plainly enough the finger of God, is that, in the narrow road cut through the rock, which still passes under the wall of the Capuchin convent, Giulio and his mistress, disguised as friars, met Signor de' Campireali and his son Fabio, who, followed by four servants well armed, and preceded by a page carrying a lighted torch, were returning from Castel Gandolfo, a town situated on the shore of the lake at no great distance. To allow the lovers to pass, the Campireali and their servants stood aside to the right and left of the road cut in the rock, which is about eight feet wide. How much better would it have been for Elena to be recognised at that moment! She would have been killed by a shot from her father's or her brother's pistol, and her punishment would have lasted but an instant: but heaven had ordered otherwise (*Dis aliter visum*).

"A further detail is added with regard to this strange encounter, which Signora de' Campireali, in her extreme old age, when almost a centenarian, used at times to relate in Rome in the presence of persons of weight, who, themselves of a great age, repeated it to me when my insatiable curiosity questioned them as to this matter and many others.

"Fabio de' Campireali, who was a young man proud of his courage and extremely arrogant, observing that the elder of the friars gave no greeting either to his father or to himself when passing so close to them, exclaimed:

" 'There's a conceited rascal of a friar! Heaven knows

[79]

what he is going to do outside his convent, he and his friend, at this time of night! I don't know why I don't pull off their cowls; we should see their faces.'

"At these words, Giulio gripped his dirk under his friar's habit, and placed himself between Fabio and Elena. At that moment he was not more than a foot away from Fabio; but heaven ordered otherwise, and by a miracle calmed the fury of these two young men, who were presently to see each other at such close quarters."

In the prosecution of Elena de' Campireali in after years, an attempt was made to present this nocturnal expedition as a proof of her corruption. It was the delirium of a young heart inflamed by a mad love, but that heart was pure.

III

IT should be explained that the Orsini, the perpetual
rivals of the Colonna, and all powerful at that time
in the villages nearest to Rome, had recently procured
the passing of a sentence of death, by the government
courts, on a rich farmer named Baldassare Bandini, a na-
tive of la Petrella. It would take too long to relate here
the various actions of which Bandini was accused: the
majority would be crimes to-day, but could not be re-
garded in so severe a fashion in 1559. Bandini was im-
prisoned in a castle belonging to the Orsini, and situated
in the mountains in the direction of Valmontone, six leagues
from Albano. The *bargello* of Rome, accompanied by one
hundred and fifty of his *sbirri,* spent a night on the road;
he was coming to fetch Bandini to take him to Rome, to
the Tordinona prison; Bandini had appealed to Rome from
the sentence which condemned him to death. But, as we
have said, he was a native of la Petrella, a fortress belong-
ing to the Colonna; Bandini's wife appeared and publicly
asked Fabrizio Colonna, who happened to be at la Petrella:
"Are you going to allow one of your faithful servants to
die?"

Colonna replied:
"May I never, please God, be wanting in the respect
I owe to the decisions of the courts of my Lord, the Pope!"

Immediately his soldiers received orders, and he sent
word to all his supporters to hold themselves in readiness.
The place of assembly was fixed in the neighbourhood of
Valmontone, a little town built on the summit of a rock
of moderate height, but with the rampart of a continuous
and almost vertical precipice of from sixty to eighty feet.

It was to this town, which belonged to the Pope, that the supporters of the Orsini and the government *sbirri* had succeeded in conveying Bandini. Among the most zealous supporters of authority were numbered Signor de' Campireali and Fabio, his son, who, moreover, were distantly related to the Orsini. Giulio Branciforte and his father, on the other hand, had always been attached to the Colonna.

In circumstances in which it did not suit the Colonna to act openly, they had recourse to a very simple stratagem: the majority of the wealthy Roman peasants, then as now, belonged to some confraternity or other of penitents. These penitents, whenever they appear in public, cover their heads with a piece of cloth which hides the face and is pierced with two holes opposite the eyes. When the Colonna did not wish to avow their part in any enterprise, they used to invite their supporters to put on their penitential dress before coming to join them.

After long preparations, the removal of Bandini, which for a fortnight had been the talk of the countryside, was fixed for a Sunday. On that day, at two o'clock in the morning, the governor of Valmontone had the bells rung in all the villages of the forest of la Faggiola. The peasants were to be seen emerging in considerable numbers from each village. (The customs of the mediaeval Republics, when one fought to obtain a certain thing which one desired, had preserved a great element of courage in the peasant heart; in these days, no one would stir.)

On the day in question a curious thing might have been observed: as the little troop of armed peasants issuing from every village reached the cover of the forest, it diminished by half; the supporters of the Colonna made their way to the place of assembly given out by Fabrizio. Their leaders appeared to be convinced that there would be no fighting that day: they had received orders that morning to spread this rumour. Fabrizio ranged the forest with the picked men of his supporters, whom he had mounted on the young and half-broken horses of his stud. He held a sort of review of the various detachments of peasants; but he said nothing to any of them, as a single word might prove compromising. Fabrizio was a large, lean man, of an incredible agility and strength: although barely forty-five years old, his hair and moustache were dazzlingly white, which greatly annoyed him: by this peculiarity he could be recognised in places where he would have preferred to pass unknown. As soon as the peasants caught sight of him, they cried: *"Evviva Colonna!"* and put on their cloth hoods. The Prince himself had his hood hanging over his chest, so as to be able to draw it on as soon as he came in sight of the enemy.

Which enemy did not keep him waiting: the sun had scarcely risen when about a thousand men, belonging to the Orsini party, and coming from the direction of Valmontone, entered the forest and passed within some three hundred yards of the supporters of Fabrizio Colonna, who had made his men lie down. A few minutes after the last of the Orsini troops forming this advance guard had filed past, the Prince ordered his men to move; he had decided to attack Bandini's escort a quarter of an hour after it should have entered the wood. At this point the forest is littered with small rocks fifteen or twenty feet high; these are waves of lava, more or less ancient, on which the chestnuts flourish admirably, and almost entirely shut out the light of day. As these drifts of lava, more or less eaten away by time, make the ground very uneven, to avoid making the high road pass over a number of unnecessary little gradients, the lava has been cut into, and very often the road runs three or four feet below the level of the forest.

Near the place chosen by Fabrizio for the attack, was

a clearing covered with vegetation and crossed at one end by the high road. Beyond this the road again entered the forest, which, at this point, choked with brambles and shrubs between the trunks of the trees, was altogether impenetrable. It was at a point a hundred paces within the forest and on either side of the road that Fabrizio posted his men. At a signal from the Prince, each of the peasants arranged his hood, and took his post with his arquebus behind a chestnut; the Prince's soldiers placed themselves behind the trees nearest to the road. The peasants had a definite order to fire only after the soldiers, and these were not to open fire until the enemy should be within twenty paces. Fabrizio made them hastily fell a score of trees, which, flung down with their branches upon the road, fairly narrow at that point and three feet below the level of the forest, blocked it entirely. Captain Ranuccio, with five hundred men, followed the advance guard; he had orders not to attack it until he should hear the first arquebus shots fired from the barricade that blocked the road. When Fabrizio Colonna saw his troops and the rest of his supporters properly posted, each behind his tree, and full of determination, he set off at a gallop with all those of his men who were mounted, among whom was to be seen Giulio Branciforte. The Prince took a path to the right of the high road, which led to the farther end of the clearing.

He had been gone but a few minutes when his men saw approaching in the distance, by the road from Valmontone, a numerous troop of men on horseback; these were the *sbirri* and the *bargello*, escorting Bandini, and the whole of the Orsini horsemen. In their midst was Baldassare Bandini, surrounded by four executioners clothed in red; they had orders to carry out the sentence of the court of first instance and to put Bandini to death, if they saw the supporters of the Colonna attempting to set him free.

Colonna's cavalry had barely arrived at the end of the clearing or meadow furthest from the road, when he heard the first arquebus shots fired by the ambuscade which he had posted on the high road by the barricade. Immediately he ordered his horsemen to gallop, and made them charge upon the four executioners clothed in red who surrounded Bandini.

We shall not attempt to follow the narrative of this little affair, which was over in three quarters of an hour; the Orsini party, taken by surprise, scattered in all directions, but, in the advance guard, the gallant Captain Ranuccio was killed, an event which had a fatal influence on the destiny of Branciforte. Barely had the latter dealt a few sabre thrusts, as he made his way towards the four men clothed in red, before he found himself face to face with Fabio de' Campireali.

Mounted upon a fiery horse, and wearing a gilded *giacco* (a coat of mail), Fabio cried:

"Who are these wretched creatures in masks? Cut their masks off with your sabres; this is how I do it!"

A moment later, Giulio Branciforte received a horizontal slash from Fabio's sabre across his brow. This blow had been so skilfully aimed that the cloth which covered his face fell to the ground, while at the same time his eyes were blinded by the blood that flowed from his wound, though the latter was not at all serious. Giulio reined in his horse, to give himself time to breathe and to wipe his face. He was anxious, at all costs, not to fight with Elena's brother; and his horse was already four paces from Fabio when he received a furious sabre thrust on the chest, which did not enter his body, thanks to his *giacco*, but did take away his breath for a moment. At the same time a voice shouted in his ear:

"*Ti conosco, porco!* I know you, you swine! So this is how you make money to replace your tatters!"

Giulio, stung to anger, forgot his original intention and turned on Fabio:

"*Ed in mal punto venisti!*" [1] he cried.

After a succession of vigorous blows the garments that covered their coats of mail fell off in tatters. Fabio's coat of mail was gilded and splendid, Giulio's of the commonest kind.

"In what gutter did you pick up your *giacco?*" Fabio cried to him.

At that moment, Giulio found the opportunity which he had been seeking for the last half minute: Fabio's superb coat of mail did not fit closely enough round his throat, and Giulio aimed at his throat, which was bare in one place, a thrust that went home. Giulio's sword ran six inches into Fabio's breast, causing a huge jet of blood to spout forth.

"Take that for your insolence!" cried Giulio.

And he galloped towards the men dressed in red, two of whom were still in the saddle a hundred yards away. As he approached them, a third fell; but, just as Giulio came up to the fourth executioner, the latter, seeing himself surrounded by more than ten horsemen, fired a pistol point blank at the unfortunate Baldassare Bandini, who fell.

"Now, gentlemen, there is nothing more for us to do here!" cried Branciforte. "Let us sabre these rascals of *sbirri* who are making off everywhere."

The others all followed him.

When, half an hour later, Giulio rejoined Fabrizio Colonna, that nobleman addressed him for the first time in his life. Giulio found him mad with rage; he had expected to see him in a transport of joy, in view of the victory, which was complete and due entirely to his good

[1] "And you have come at an unlucky moment!"

arrangement; for the Orsini had nearly three thousand
men, and Fabrizio, on this occasion, had not been able to
muster more than fifteen hundred.

"We have lost our gallant friend Ranuccio!" the Prince
exclaimed, addressing Giulio. "I have just touched his
body myself; it is cold already. Poor Baldassare Bandini
is mortally wounded. So, properly speaking, we have not
been successful. But the ghost of the gallant Captain
Ranuccio will appear before Pluto with a good escort. I
have given orders to hang all these rascally prisoners from
the branches of the trees. Do your duty, gentlemen," he
cried, raising his voice.

And he went off again at a gallop to the place where the
advance guard had been engaged. Giulio had been more
or less second in command of Ranuccio's company; he fol-
lowed the Prince, who, on coming up to the body of that
brave soldier, which lay surrounded by more than fifty of
the enemy's dead, dismounted a second time to take
Ranuccio's hand. Giulio followed his example, with tears
in his eyes.

"You are very young," the Prince said to him, "but I
see you covered with blood, and your father was a brave
man, who received more than a score of wounds in the
service of the Colonna. Take command of what is left
of Ranuccio's company, and carry his body to our church
of la Petrella; remember that you may perhaps be attacked
on the way."

Giulio was not attacked, but he killed with a stroke of
his sword one of his own men, who said that he was too
young to be in command. This rash act proved success-
ful, because Giulio was still covered with Fabio's blood.
All along the road, he found the trees loaded with men
who were being hanged. This hideous spectacle, combined
with the death of Ranuccio, and more especially with that

of Fabio, drove him almost mad. His only hope was that the name of Fabio's conqueror would remain unknown.

We pass over the military details. Three days after the battle, he was able to return to spend a few hours at Albano; he told his friends there that a violent fever had detained him in Rome, where he had been obliged to keep his bed all the week.

But he was treated everywhere with a marked respect; the most important persons of the town made haste to greet him; some rash fellows even went so far as to call him *Signor Capitano*. He had passed several times in front of the palazzo Campireali, which he found entirely shut up, and, as the newly made Captain was extremely shy when it came to asking certain questions, it was not until the middle of the day that he managed to take it upon himself to say to Scotti, an old man who had always treated him kindly:

"But where are the Campireali? I see their palazzo shut up."

"My friend," replied Scotti with a sudden grimness, "that is a name which you must never utter. Your friends are quite convinced that it was he who attacked you, and they will say so everywhere; but, after all, he was the chief obstacle to your marriage; after all, his death leaves his sister immensely rich, and she is in love with you. It may even be added, and indiscretion becomes a virtue at this moment, it may even be added that she loves you to the extent of going to pay you a visit at night in your little house at Alba. So it may be said, in your interest, that you were husband and wife before the fatal combat at the Ciampi." (This was the name given in the district to the fight which we have described.)

The old man broke off, because he saw that Giulio was in tears.

"Let us go up to the inn," said Giulio.

Scotti followed him; they were given a room the door
of which they locked, and Giulio asked the old man's leave
to tell him everything that had happened in the last week.
This long story finished:

"I can see quite well from your tears," said the old
man, "that nothing in your conduct was premeditated; but
Fabio's death is none the less a very terrible event for you.
It is absolutely essential that Elena tells her mother that
you have been her husband for some time."

Giulio made no reply; this the old man ascribed to a
praiseworthy discretion. Absorbed in deep meditation,
Giulio was asking himself whether Elena, enraged by the
death of a brother, would do justice to his delicacy; he
repented of what had happened before. Afterwards, at
his request, the old man told him frankly of everything
that had occurred in Albano on the day of the fight.
Fabio having been killed about half past six in the morn-
ing, more than six leagues from Albano, incredible as it
might sound, by nine o'clock people had begun to speak
of his death. Towards midday they had seen old Cam-
pireali, in floods of tears and supported by his servants,
making his way to· the Capuchin convent. Shortly after-
wards, three of those good fathers, mounted on the best
horses of the Campireali stable, and followed by a num-
ber of servants, had taken the road to the village of the
Ciampi, in the neighbourhood of which the battle had been
fought. Old Campireali was absolutely determined to ac-
company them; but he had been dissuaded, on the grounds
that Fabrizio Colonna was furious (no one knew why)
and might easily do him an ill turn should he be taken
prisoner.

That evening, towards midnight, the forest of la Fag-
giola had seemed to be on fire: this was all the monks and
all the poor of Albano who, each carrying a huge lighted
candle, went out to meet the body of young Fabio.

"I shall not conceal from you," the old man went on, lowering his voice as though he had been afraid of being overheard, "that the road which leads to Valmontone and to the Ciampi. . . ."

"Well?" said Giulio.

"Well, that road passes by your house, and they say that when Fabio's body reached that point, the blood gushed out from a horrible wound which he had in his throat."

"How terrible!" cried Giulio, springing to his feet.

"Calm yourself, my friend," said the old man, "you can see for yourself that you must know all. And now I may tell you that your presence here, to-day, has seemed a trifle premature. If you should do me the honour to consult me, I should add, Captain, that it is not advisable for you to appear in Albano for another month. I have no need to warn you that it would not be prudent to shew yourself in Rome. We do not yet know what course the Holy Father is going to adopt towards the Colonna; it is thought that he will accept the statement of Fabrizio, who professes that he heard of the fight at the Ciampi only from common rumour; but the Governor of Rome, who is out and out Orsini, is furious and would be only too glad to have one of Fabrizio's gallant soldiers hanged, nor would Fabrizio himself have any reasonable grounds for complaint, since he swears that he took no part in the fight. I shall go farther, and, although you have not asked me for it, take the liberty of giving you a piece of military advice: you are popular in Albano, otherwise you would not be able to stay here in safety. Bear in mind that you have been walking about the town for some hours, that one of the Orsini's supporters might imagine that you were defying him, or at least think it an easy opportunity of winning a fine reward. Old Campireali has repeated a thousand times that he will give his richest estate to whoever kills you. You ought to have brought down to Albano some of the soldiers you have in your house."

"I have no soldiers in my house."

"In that case, Captain, you are mad. This inn has a garden, we are going to leave by the garden, and escape through the vineyards. I shall accompany you; I am an old man, and unarmed; but if we meet any ill-disposed persons, I shall talk to them, and at least be able to let you gain time."

Giulio was broken-hearted. Dare we mention the nature of his madness? As soon as he had learned that the palazzo Campireali was shut up and that its occupants had left for Rome, he had formed the plan of going to revisit that garden where so often he had conversed with Elena. He even hoped to see once again her bedroom, where he had been received when her mother was away. He felt the need of reassuring himself against her anger, by the sight of the places in which she had been so loving to him.

Branciforte and the chivalrous old man met with no misadventure as they followed the little paths that run through the vineyards and climb towards the lake.

Giulio made his companion tell him once more the details of young Fabio's burial. The body of that gallant young man, escorted by a crowd of priests, had been taken to Rome, and buried in the chapel of his family, in the Convent of Sant' Onofrio, on the summit of the Janiculum. It had been observed, as something extremely unusual, that, on the eve of the ceremony, Elena had been taken back by her father to the Convent of the Visitation, at Castro; this had confirmed the common report which insisted that she was secretly married to the soldier of fortune who had had the misfortune to kill her brother.

On nearing his own house, Giulio found the corporal of

his company and four of his men; they told him that their old captain used never to leave the forest without having some of his men at hand. The Prince had said many times that, whenever anyone wished to have himself killed by his own rashness, he must first resign his commission, so as not to cast upon him the responsibility for avenging another death.

Giulio Branciforte realised the soundness of these ideas, of which until that moment he had been completely ignorant. He had supposed, as young nations suppose, that war consisted only in fighting with personal courage. He at once complied with the Prince's wishes, only giving himself time to embrace the wise old man who had been so chivalrous as to accompany him to his house.

But, not many days later, Giulio, half mad with melancholy, returned to visit the palazzo Campireali. As night was falling, he and three of his men, disguised as Neapolitan merchants, made their way into Albano. He presented himself alone at the house of Scotti; he learned that Elena was still confined in the convent of Castro. Her father, who believed her to be married to the man whom he called his son's murderer, had sworn never to set eyes on her again. He had not seen her even when he was taking her to the convent. Her mother's affection seemed, on the contrary, to have increased, and she often left Rome to go and spend a day or two with her daughter.

IV

"IF I do not justify myself to Elena," Giulio told himself as he made his way back, by night, to the quarters which his company were occupying in the forest, "she will come to regard me as a murderer. Heaven knows what stories they have been telling her about this fatal fight!"

He went to receive his orders from the Prince in his stronghold of la Petrella, and asked leave to go to Castro. Fabrizio Colonna frowned:

"The matter of the little disturbance is not yet settled with His Holiness. You must understand that I have told the truth, namely that I knew nothing whatever of that encounter, of which I was not even informed until the following day, here, in my castle of la Petrella. I have every reason to believe that His Holiness will finally accept this sincere statement. But the Orsini are powerful, and everybody is saying that you distinguished yourself in the skirmish. The Orsini go so far as to pretend that a number of prisoners were hanged from the branches of the trees. You know how little truth there is in that; but we may expect reprisals."

The profound astonishment revealed in the young captain's artless gaze amused the Prince: he decided, however, seeing such a display of innocence, that it would be as well to speak more plainly.

"I see in you," he went on, "that absolute bravery which has made the name of Branciforte famous throughout Italy. I hope that you will shew that loyalty towards

[93]

my house which made your father so dear to me, and which I have sought to reward in you. The standing order among my troops is this: never tell the truth about anything that relates to me or to my men. If, at the moment when you are obliged to speak, you see no advantage in any particular falsehood, lie at random, and avoid as you would avoid a mortal sin ever uttering a word of the truth. You can understand that, taken in conjunction with other information, it may put people on the track of my plans. I know, as it happens, that you have a little love affair in the convent at Castro; you may go and waste a fortnight in that town, where the Orsini are certain to have friends, and even agents. Call on my steward, who will pay you two hundred sequins. The affection that I had for your father," the Prince added with a smile, "prompts me to give you a few instructions as to the best way of carrying out this amorous and military undertaking. You and three of your men will be disguised as merchants; you will not forget to lose your temper with one of your companions, who will make a show of being always drunk, and will make plenty of friends for himself by standing wine to all the vagabonds of Castro. . . . Apart from that," the Prince went on, with a change of tone, "if you are taken by the Orsini and put to death, never confess your true name, still less that you belong to me. I have no need to advise you to make a circuit of all the small towns, and always to enter by the gate farthest from the road by which you arrive."

Giulio's heart was melted by this fatherly advice, coming from a man who was ordinarily so solemn. At first the Prince smiled at the tears which he saw gathering in the young man's eyes; then his own voice altered. He slipped off one of the many rings which he wore on his fingers; as he took it, Giulio kissed that hand, famous for so many great deeds.

"My father would never have told me so much," the young man cried enthusiastically.

Two days later, shortly before dawn, he passed within the walls of the small town of Castro; five soldiers followed him, disguised like himself: two of them kept to themselves and appeared not to know either him or the other three. Even before entering the town, Giulio caught sight of the Convent of the Visitation, a vast building surrounded by dark walls, and not unlike a fortress. He hastened to the church, which was magnificent. The nuns, all of them noble and mostly belonging to wealthy families, competed among themselves in their pride for the privilege of enriching this church, the only part of the convent that was exposed to the public gaze. It had become a custom that whichever of these ladies the Pope appointed Abbess, from a list of three names presented to him by the Cardinal Protector of the Order of the Visitation, made a considerable offering, intended to perpetuate her name. Any whose offering was inferior to that of the previous Abbess was despised, and her family as well.

Giulio made his way trembling through this magnificent building, resplendent with marble and gilding. As a matter of fact, he paid little attention to the marble or the gilding; he felt that Elena's eyes were upon him. The high altar, he was told, had cost more than eight hundred thousand francs; but his gaze, scorning the treasures of the high altar, was directed at a gilded grating, nearly forty feet high, and divided into three sections by a pair of marble pillars. This grating, whose vast mass made it appear almost terrifying, rose behind the high altar, and separated the nuns' choir from the church itself, which was open to all the faithful.

Giulio told himself that behind this gilded grating were assembled, during the services, the nuns and their boarders. To this inner church might repair, at any hour of the day, a nun or a boarder who felt a desire to pray; it was upon this circumstance, known to the world at large, that the poor lover's hopes were based.

It was true that an immense black curtain screened the inner side of the grating; but "that curtain," thought Giulio, "cannot entirely block the view for the boarders when they look into the public church, since I, who am unable to approach within a certain distance of it, can see quite well, through the curtain, the windows that light the choir, and can even make out the smallest architectural details." Each bar of this magnificent grating was armed with a strong spike, pointed towards the worshippers.

Giulio chose a place where he would be clearly visible, opposite the left hand side of the grating, in the most brightly lighted part of the church; there he spent his time hearing masses. As he saw no one near him but peasants, he had hopes of being observed, even through the black curtain which draped the inside of the grating. For the first time in his life, this simple young man sought to create an effect; he dressed himself with care; he scattered alms broadcast as he entered and left the church. His men and himself paid endless attentions to all the workmen and small tradesmen who had any dealings with the convent. It was not, however, until the third day that he at last had hopes of conveying a letter to Elena. By his orders, his men closely followed the two lay sisters whose duty it was to purchase some of the provisions for the convent; one of them was on friendly terms with a small merchant. One of Giulio's soldiers, who had been in religion, made friends with this merchant, and promised him a sequin for each letter that should be conveyed to the boarder Elena de' Campireali.

"What!" said the merchant at the first overture that

was made to him in the matter, "a letter to the *brigand's wife!*"

This name was already in common use in Castro, and Elena had not been there a fortnight: so swiftly does anything that seizes hold of the imagination circulate among this people, passionately interested in all exact details! The merchant added:

"At least, she is married! But how many of our ladies have not that excuse, and yet receive a great deal more than letters from outside."

In this first letter, Giulio related with endless details everything that had occurred on the fatal day marked by the death of Fabio: "Do you hate me?" he said in conclusion.

Elena replied in a few lines that, without hating anyone, she was going to employ the rest of her life in trying to forget the man by whose hand her brother had perished.

Giulio made haste to reply; after inveighing against his fate, in a style imitated from Plato and in fashion at the time:

"So you wish," he went on, "to forget the Word of God handed down to us in the Holy Scriptures? God says: woman shall leave her family and her parents to follow her husband. Dare you pretend that you are not my wife? Remember the night of Saint Peter's day. As dawn was beginning to appear behind Monte Cavi, you flung yourself at my feet; I was good enough to grant you a respite; you were mine, had I wished to take you; you could not resist the love which you then felt for me. Suddenly it occurred to me that, as I had told you many times that I had long since offered you the sacrifice of my life and of all that I might hold most dear in the world, you were in a position to reply, although you never did, that all these sacrifices, not being marked by any outward action, might well be no more than imaginary. An idea, hard to bear, but fundamentally just, dawned upon me. I reflected that it was not for nothing that chance was presenting me with the opportunity of sacrificing in your interest the greatest happiness that I could ever have dreamed of. You were already in my arms, and defenceless, remember; your own lips dared not refuse. At that moment the morning Angelus rang from the convent of Monte Cavi, and, by a miracle, the sound reached our ears. You said to me: 'Make this sacrifice to the Holy Madonna, the mother of all purity.' I had already, a moment earlier, had the idea of this supreme sacrifice, the only real sacrifice that I should ever have an opportunity of making for you. I felt it strange that the same idea should have occurred to you. The distant sound of that Angelus touched me, I confess; I granted your request. The sacrifice was not entirely for you; I believed that I was placing our future union under the protection of the Madonna. At that time I supposed that the objections would come not from you, faithless one, but from your rich and noble family. Had there not been some supernatural intervention, how could that Angelus have reached our ears from so great a distance, carried over the treetops of half the forest, stirred at that moment by the morning breeze? Then, you remember, you threw yourself at my feet; I rose, I took from my bosom the cross which I carry there, and you swore upon that cross, which is here before me, and by your own eternal damnation, that in whatever place you might at any time be, whatever might at any time happen, as soon as I should give you the order, you would place yourself entirely at my disposal, as you were at the moment when the Angelus from Monte Cavi travelled so far to strike your ear. We then repeated devoutly two *Hail Marys* and two *Our Fathers*. Very well, by the love which you then felt for me, or else, if you have forgotten it, as I fear, by your eternal damnation, I order you to receive me to-night, in your room or in the garden of the Convent of the Visitation."

The Italian author carefully reports many long letters written by Giulio Branciforte after this one; but he gives only extracts from the replies of Elena de' Campireali. After the lapse of two hundred and seventy-eight years, we are so remote from the sentiments of love and religion which fill these letters, that I have been afraid of their seeming wearisome.

It appears from these letters that Elena finally obeyed the order contained in this one, of which we have given an abridged translation. Giulio found a way of penetrating into the convent; we may conclude from a certain passage that he disguised himself as a woman. Elena received him, but only at the grating of a window on the ground floor looking out to the garden. To his unspeakable grief, Giulio found that this girl, so tender and indeed so passionate before, had become like a stranger to him; she treated him almost with *civility*. In admitting him to the garden, she had yielded almost exclusively to the obligation of her oath. Their meeting was brief: after a few moments, Giulio's pride, excited a little, perhaps, by the events that had occurred in the last fortnight, succeeded in prevailing over his intense grief.

"I see before me now," he said to himself, "only the tomb of that Elena who, at Albano, seemed to have given herself to me for life."

Immediately, the important thing for Giulio was to conceal the tears with which the polite turns of speech that Elena adopted in addressing him bathed his cheeks. When she had finished speaking and justifying a change that was so natural, she said, after the death of a brother, Giulio said to her, speaking very slowly:

"You are not abiding by your oath, you do not receive

me in a garden, you are not on your knees before me,
as you were for a minute after we had heard the Angelus
from Monte Cavi. Forget your oath if you can; as for
me, I forget nothing; may God help you!"

So saying, he left the barred window before which he
might still have remained for nearly an hour. Who would
have said, a moment earlier, that he would of his own
free will cut short this meeting for which he had so longed!
This sacrifice rent his heart; but he felt that he might
well deserve Elena's scorn if he replied to her *civilities*
otherwise than by abandoning her to her own remorse.

Before dawn, he left the convent. At once he mounted
his horse, giving orders to his men to wait for him at
Castro for a full week, then to return to the forest. At
first he rode towards Rome.

"What! I am going away from her!" he said to him-
self at every yard: "What! We have become strangers to
one another! Oh, Fabio! How amply you are avenged!"

The sight of the men whom he passed on the road in-
creased his anger; he urged his horse across country and
made his way towards the deserted and uncultivated tract
by the seashore. When he was no longer disturbed by
meeting these placid peasants whose lot he envied, he drew
breath; the aspect of this wild spot was in keeping with
his despair and lessened his rage; then he was able to give
himself up to the consideration of his sad fate.

"At my age," he said to himself, "I have one resource
left: to love some other woman!"

At this melancholy thought, he felt his despair increase
twofold; he saw only too clearly that there was for him
but one woman in the world. He pictured to himself the
torment that he would suffer should he venture to utter
the word love to any woman but Elena: the idea tore his
heart.

He was seized with a fit of bitter laughter.

"Here I am," he thought, "exactly like those heroes in
Ariosto who travel alone through desert lands, when they
have to forget that they have found their mistress in the
arms of some other knight. . . . And yet she is not so
much to blame," he told himself, bursting into tears after
this fit of wild laughter; "her faithlessness does not reach
the point of loving another. That keen, pure spirit has
allowed herself to be led astray by the dreadful accounts
that have been given her of me; no doubt I have been rep-
resented to her as having armed myself for that fatal ex-
pedition only in the secret hope of finding an opportunity
of killing her brother. They will have gone farther still:
they will have credited me with the sordid calculation that
once her brother was dead she would become the sole
heiress of an immense property. . . . And I have been
fool enough to leave her for a whole fortnight a prey to
the wiles of my enemies! It must be admitted that if I
am most unfortunate, heaven has also furnished me with
singularly little sense with which to conduct my life! I
am a most miserable, most contemptible creature! My
life has been of use to no one, and to myself least of all."

At that moment, young Branciforte had an inspiration
very rare in that age: his horse was going along the water's
edge, and every now and then was being splashed by the
waves; he had the idea of urging the animal into the sea,
and so ending the dreadful fate that overhung him. What
was he to do henceforward, after the one person in the
world who had ever made him feel the existence of hap-
piness had abandoned him? Then suddenly another idea
stopped him short.

"What are the pains that I am enduring," he said to
himself, "compared with those which I shall suffer in a
moment, once this wretched life is ended? Elena will no
longer be simply indifferent to me, as she is in reality;
I shall see her in the arms of a rival, and that rival will

be some young Roman noble, rich and *highly esteemed;* for, to rend my heart, the devils will seek out the most cruel visions, as is their duty. So I shall never succeed in finding forgetfulness of Elena, even in death; far from it, my passion for her will be doubled, because that is the surest means which the Eternal Power can find of punishing me for the fearful sin which I shall have committed."

To banish the temptation finally, Giulio began devoutly reciting the *Hail Mary.* It was on hearing the morning Angelus, the prayer sacred to the Madonna, that he had been carried away before, and led to a generous action which he now regarded as the greatest mistake of his life. But, from a sense of reverence, he did not venture to go farther and express the whole of the idea that had seized hold of his mind.

"If, by the Madonna's inspiration, I have fallen into a fatal error, ought she not, in her infinite justice, to bring about some circumstance which will restore my happiness?"

This idea of the justice of the Madonna gradually banished his despair. He raised his head, and saw facing him, beyond Albano and the forest, that Monte Cavi, covered in its dusky greenery, and the holy convent whose morning Angelus had led him into what he now called his appalling stupidity. The unexpected sight of that holy place comforted him.

"No!" he exclaimed; "it is impossible that the Madonna should abandon me. If Elena had been my wife, as her love allowed and my dignity as a man required, the account given to her of her brother's death would have found in her heart the memory of the bond that attached her to me. She would have told herself that she belonged to me long before the fatal chance which, on a field of battle, brought me face to face with Fabio. He was two years older than I; he was more skilled in arms, bolder in every way, stronger. A thousand reasons would have occurred to my wife to prove that it was not I that had sought that combat. She would have remembered that I had never shewn the slightest feeling of hatred towards her brother, even when he fired his arquebus at me. I can recall that at our first meeting, after my return from Rome, I said to her: 'What would you have? Honour required it; I cannot blame a brother!' "

His hope restored by his devotion to the Madonna, Giulio urged on his horse and in a few hours arrived at his company's cantonment. He found his men standing to arms: they were about to take the road that runs from Naples to Rome past Monte Cassino. The young captain changed horses, and marched with his men. There was no fighting that day. Giulio never asked himself why they were on the march; it mattered little to him. The moment that he found himself at the head of his soldiers, a new vision of his destiny appeared to him.

"I am simply and solely a fool," he said to himself; "I did wrong to leave Castro; Elena is probably less to blame than I in my anger imagined. No, she cannot have ceased to belong to me, that pure and simple heart, in which I have beheld the first dawn of love! She was steeped in so sincere a passion for me! Has she not offered, ten times and more, to fly with me, poor as I am, and to have ourselves married by one of the friars of Monte Cavi? At Castro I ought, first of all, to have obtained a second assignation, and made her listen to reason. Really, passion makes me as distracted as a child! God! Why have I not a friend to whom I can turn for advice! The same course of action seems to me execrable, and, the next minute, excellent."

On the evening of that day, as they left the high road to return to the forest, Giulio rode up to the Prince and asked whether he might stay for a few days longer at the place he knew of.

"You can go to the devil!" cried Fabrizio, "do you think this is the time to bother me with your childish nonsense?"

An hour later, Giulio set off again for Castro. He found his men there, but he did not know how to write to Elena, after the summary fashion in which he had left her. His first letter contained only these words: "May I be received to-morrow evening?"

Similarly, *"You may come,"* was all the answer he received.

After Giulio's departure, Elena had imagined herself to be abandoned for ever. Then she had felt the whole force of the argument urged by that poor young man who was so unhappy: she was his wife before he had had the misfortune to encounter her brother on a field of battle.

On this occasion, Giulio was by no means received with the polite turns of speech which had struck him as so cruel at their former meeting. It was true that Elena appeared to him only behind the shelter of her barred window; but she was trembling, and as Giulio was extremely reserved and his language [1] almost that which he would have used to address a stranger, it was Elena's turn to feel all the cruelty that exists in the almost official tone when it follows the most tender intimacy. Giulio, who was especially afraid of having his soul torn asunder by some cold speech proceeding from Elena's heart, had adopted a lawyer's tone to prove that Elena was his wife long before the fatal combat at the Ciampi. Elena let him speak, because she was afraid of being overcome by tears if she answered him otherwise than with a few brief words. Finally, seeing that she was on the point of betraying herself, she bade her lover come again the next day. Giulio, who was

[1] In Italy the fashion of addressing a person as *tu, voi* or *Lei* marks the degree of intimacy. The word *tu,* à survival from the Latin, has a more restricted application than in France.

reasoning like a lover, left the garden deep in thought;
he could not bring his uncertainty to the point of deciding
whether he had been well or ill received; and as military
ideas, inspired by conversation with his comrades, were
beginning to take root in his brain:

"One day," he said to himself, "I shall perhaps have
to come and carry off Elena."

And he began to consider the ways of entering the gar-
den by force. As the convent was very rich and offered
grand opportunities of pillage, it had in its pay a great
number of menservants, mostly old soldiers; they were
housed in a sort of barrack the barred windows of which
overlooked the narrow passage which, from the outer gate
of the convent, carved out of a sombre wall more than eighty
feet high, led to the inner gate guarded by the portress.
On the left of this narrow passage rose the barrack, on
the right the wall of the garden, thirty feet high. The
front of the convent, on the public square, was a mas-
sive wall black with age, and offered no openings save
the outer gate and one small window through which the
soldiers could see what went on outside. One may imag-
ine the grim effect of this great black wall pierced only
by a gate strengthened with broad iron bands fastened
to it by enormous nails, and a single small window four
feet high and eighteen inches broad.

We shall not attempt to follow the author of the orig-
inal manuscript in his long account of the successive as-
signations which Giulio obtained from Elena. The tone
mutually adopted by the lovers had once more become en-
tirely intimate, as in the past in the garden at Albano;
only Elena had never consented to come down to the gar-
den. One night Giulio found her profoundly thoughtful:
her mother had come from Rome to see her, and was stay-
ing for some days in the convent. This mother was so
loving, she had always shewn such delicacy in her treat-

ment of what she supposed to be her daughter's affections, that the latter felt a profound remorse at being obliged to deceive her; for, after all, would she ever dare to tell her that she was receiving the man who had robbed her of her son? Elena ended by admitting frankly to Giulio that if this mother who was so good to her should question her in a certain way, she would never have the strength to answer her with lies. Giulio was fully aware of the danger of his position; his fate depended on the chance which might dictate certain words to Signora de' Campireali. On the following night he said to her, with a resolute air:

"To-morrow I shall come earlier, I shall detach one of the bars of this grating, you will come down to the garden, I shall take you to a church in the town, where a priest who is devoted to me will marry us. Before daylight you will be back in this garden. Once you are my wife, I shall have nothing more to fear, and if your mother insists upon it, as an expiation of the fearful misfortune which we all equally deplore, I will consent to anything, were it even that I must spend some months without seeing you."

As Elena appeared terrified by this proposal, Giulio added:

"The Prince summons me back to his side; honour and all sorts of reasons oblige me to go. My proposal is the only one that can assure our future happiness; if you do not agree to it, let us separate for ever, here, at this moment. I shall leave you with a sense of remorse at my rashness. *I trusted in your word of honour,* you are unfaithful to the most sacred of oaths, and I hope that in the course of time the contempt which your fickleness rightly inspires in me may cure me of this love which has been for too long the bane of my life."

Elena burst into tears:

"Great God!" she exclaimed, weeping, "how terrible
for my mother!"

In the end, she agreed to the proposal that had been
made to her.

"But," she added, "some one may see us, going or com-
ing; think of the scandal that would arise, consider the
fearful position in which my mother would find herself
placed; let us wait until she goes, which will be in a few
days."

"You have succeeded in making me doubt what was to
me the holiest, the most sacred thing in the world; my con-
fidence in your word. To-morrow night we will be mar-
ried, or else we see one another now for the last time, on
this side of the grave."

Poor Elena could make no answer save by her tears,
her heart was torn especially by the cruel and decided tone
which Giulio had adopted. Had she then really merited
his contempt? Could this be that same lover who was
formerly so docile and so tender? At length she agreed
to what had been ordered of her. Giulio withdrew. From
that moment, Elena awaited the coming of the following
night in an alternation of the most rending anxieties. Had
she been prepared for certain death, her anguish would
have been less keen; she could have found some encour-
agement in the thought of Giulio's love and of her moth-
er's tender affection. The rest of that night passed in the
most agonising changes of mind. There were moments
when she decided to tell her mother all. Next day, she
was so pale when she appeared in her mother's presence,
that the latter, forgetting all her wise resolutions, flung
herself upon her daughter's bosom, crying:

"What is happening? Great God! Tell me what you
have done, or what you are going to do? If you were
to take a dagger and thrust it into my heart, you would

hurt me less than by this cruel silence which I see you adopt with me."

Her mother's intense affection was so evident to Elena, she saw so clearly that her mother, instead of exaggerating her feelings, was seeking to moderate her expression of them, that in the end she was overcome; she fell at her feet. Her mother, who was trying to find out what the fatal secret might be, having exclaimed that Elena was shunning her society, Elena replied that, next day and every day after that, she would spend all her time with her, but she besought her not to question her further.

This indiscreet utterance was speedily followed by a full confession. Signora de' Campireali was horrified to hear that her son's murderer was so close at hand. But this grief was followed by an outburst of keen and pure joy. Who could describe her delight when she learned that her daughter had never failed in her duties?

Immediately all the plans of this prudent mother were completely changed; she felt herself entitled to employ a stratagem to outwit a man who was nothing to her. Elena's heart was torn by the most cruel impulses of passion: the sincerity of her confession could not have been greater; this tormented soul was in need of relief. Signora de' Campireali, who had begun to think that anything was permissible, devised a chain of reasoning too long to be reported here. She had no difficulty in proving to her unhappy daughter that, instead of a clandestine marriage, which always leaves a stain upon a woman's reputation, she would obtain a public and perfectly honourable marriage, if she would only agree to postpone for a week the act of obedience which she owed to so high-minded a lover.

Signora de' Campireali herself would return to Rome; she would explain to her husband that, long before the fatal combat at the Ciampi, Elena had been married to Giulio. The ceremony had been performed on that very night

when, disguised in a religious habit, she had met her father
and brother by the shore of the lake, on the road cut
through the rock which runs by the walls of the Capuchin
convent. The mother took good care not to leave her
daughter all that day, and finally, towards evening, Elena
wrote her lover an ingenuous and, to our ideas, extremely
touching letter, in which she told him of the inward strug-
gle that had torn her heart. She ended by begging him
on her knees for a week's respite: "As I write you,"
she added, "this letter for which a messenger of my moth-
er's is waiting, it seems to me that I was utterly wrong
to tell her everything. I think I see you angry, your eyes
look at me with hatred; my heart is torn by the most cruel
remorse. You will say that I have a very weak, very
cowardly, very contemptible nature; I admit it, my dear
angel. But try to imagine the scene: my mother, in floods
of tears, was almost at my feet. Then it became impos-
sible for me not to tell her that a certain reason prevented
me from consenting to do what she asked; and, once I had
been so weak as to utter those rash words, I do not know
what change occurred in me, but it became almost impos-
sible for me not to tell her everything that had passed
between us. So far as I can remember, I felt that my
heart, robbed of all its strength, stood in need of advice.
This I hoped to find in a mother's words. . . . I forgot,
my friend, that that beloved mother had an interest op-
posed to yours. I forgot my first duty, which is to obey
you, and apparently I am incapable of feeling true love,
which is said to withstand every trial. Despise me, my
Giulio; but, in God's name, do not cease to love me. Carry
me off if you wish, but do me the justice to admit that, if
my mother had not happened to be here in the convent, the
most horrible dangers, shame itself, nothing in the world
could have prevented me from obeying your orders. But
that mother is so good; so clever; so generous; remember

what I told you at the time; when my father burst into
my room, she rescued your letters which I had no means
of hiding: then, when the danger was over, she gave them
back to me without wishing to read them, and without a
single word of reproach! In the same way, all my life
long, she has been to me, as she was at that moment, su-
preme. You can see whether I ought to love her, and yet,
when I write to you (it is a horrible thing to say) I feel
that I hate her. She has announced that on account of
the heat she wishes to spend the night in a tent in the
garden; I hear the tapping of the mallets, they are putting
up the tent now; impossible for us to meet to-night. I
am even afraid that the boarders' dormitory may be locked,
as well as the two doors of the spiral staircase, a thing
which is never done. These precautions would make it
impossible for me to come down to the garden, even if
I thought that it would have any effect in calming your
anger. Oh, how I would give myself to you at this mo-
ment, if I had the means! How I should run to that
church where they are going to marry us!"

This letter concludes with a couple of pages of mad
sentences, in which I notice certain impassioned arguments
which seem to be imitated from the philosophy of Plato. I
have suppressed several elegances of this sort in the letter
I have just translated.

Giulio Branciforte was amazed when he received it about
an hour before the evening Angelus; he had just com-
pleted his arrangements with the priest. He was beside
himself with rage.

"She has no need to advise me to carry her off, the weak,
cowardly creature!"

And he set off at once for the forest of la Faggiola.

Meanwhile, Signora de' Campireali's position was as
follows: her husband lay on his deathbed, the impossibility
of avenging himself on Branciforte was carrying him

slowly to the grave. In vain had he made his agents
offer considerable sums to Roman *bravi;* none of these was
prepared to attack one of the *caporali,* as they were called,
of Prince Colonna; they were too certain of being ex-
terminated, themselves and their families. It was not a
year since an entire village had been burned to punish
the death of one of Colonna's soldiers, and all those of the
inhabitants, men and women alike, who tried to flee into
the country, had their hands and feet tied together with
ropes, and were then tossed into the blazing houses.

Signora de' Campireali had large estates in the King-
dom of Naples; her husband had ordered her to send there
for assassins, but she had made only a show of obedience:
she imagined her daughter to be irrevocably bound to
Giulio Branciforte. Acting on this supposition, she
thought that Giulio should go and serve for a campaign or
two in the Spanish armies, which were then making war
on the rebels in Flanders. If he survived, that would,
she thought, be a sign that God did not disapprove of a
necessary marriage; in that case she would give her daugh-
ter the estates which she owned in the Kingdom of Naples;
Giulio Branciforte would take the name of one of these
estates, and would go with his wife to spend a few years
in Spain. After all these trials perhaps she would have
the heart to see him. But the whole aspect of things had
been changed by her daughter's confession: the marriage
was no longer a necessity: far from it, and while Elena
was writing her lover the letter which we have trans-
lated, Signora de' Campireali wrote to Pescara and
Chieti, ordering her farmers to send to her at Castro a
party of trustworthy men capable of a bold stroke. She
did not conceal from them that it was a question of aveng-
ing the death of Fabio, their young master. The courier
who conveyed these letters set off before the end of the
day.

V

BUT, two days later, Giulio was back in Castro, bringing with him eight of his men who had volunteered to follow him and expose themselves to the anger of the Prince, who had sometimes punished with death enterprises of the sort on which they were engaging. Giulio had five men at Castro, he arrived with eight more; and yet fourteen soldiers, however brave, seemed to him insufficient for his task, for the convent was like a fortress.

One had first to pass, by force or by guile, through the outer gate of the convent; then to proceed along a passage more than fifty yards in length. On the left, as has been said, rose the barred windows of a sort of barrack in which the nuns had placed thirty or forty menservants, old soldiers. From these barred windows a hot fire would be opened as soon as the alarm should be given.

The reigning Abbess, who had a head on her shoulders, was afraid of the exploits of the Orsini chiefs, Prince Colonna, Marco Sciarra, and all the others that held sway in the neighbourhood. How was one to hold out against eight hundred determined men, suddenly occupying a little town like Castro and imagining the convent to be full of gold?

As a rule, the Visitation of Castro had fifteen or twenty *bravi* in the barrack to the left of the passage which led to the inner gate of the convent; on the right of this passage was a great wall, impossible to break through; at the

end of the passage one came upon an iron gate opening
upon a pillared hall; beyond this hall was the great court-
yard of the convent. This iron gate was guarded by the
portress.

When Giulio, followed by his eight men, had come within
three leagues of Castro, he halted in a lonely inn until the
heat of the day should be past. It was only there that
he announced his intention; he then traced in the dust of
the courtyard the plan of the convent which he was going
to attack.

"At nine o'clock this evening," he said to his men, "we
sup outside the town; at midnight we enter; we shall find
your five comrades who will be waiting for us near the
convent. One of them, who will be mounted, will pretend
to be a courier arriving from Rome to summon Signora
de' Campireali to the bedside of her husband, who is dying.
We shall try to get without noise past the outer gate of
the convent, which is there, close to the barrack," he said,
pointing to it on his plan in the dust. "If we were to
begin our fight at the first gate, we should be making it
easy for the nuns' *bravi* to shoot us down with their arque-
buses while we were still in the little square, here, outside
the convent, or while we were going along the narrow pas-
sage which leads from the first gate to the second. This
second gate is of iron, but I have the key.

"It is true that there are enormous iron rods, or valets,
fastened to the wall at one end, and these, when they are
in position, prevent the two halves of the gate from open-
ing. But as these two iron rods are too heavy for the
portress to be able to handle them, I have never seen them
in position; and yet I have passed ten times and more
through this iron gate. I expect to pass through it again
to-night without difficulty. You understand that I have
friends inside the convent; my object is to carry off a
boarder, not a nun; we must not use our arms except in

the last extremity. If we should begin the fight before reaching this second gate with the iron bars, the portress would not fail to call two old gardeners, men of seventy, who sleep inside the convent, and the old men would fix in position the iron bars of which I have spoken. Should this misfortune befall us, we shall be obliged, in order to pass the gate, to destroy the wall, which will take ten minutes; in any case, I shall advance first towards the gate. One of the gardeners is in my pay; but I have taken good care, as you can imagine, not to speak to him of the abduction I have in mind. Once past this second gate, we turn to the right, and come to the garden; as soon as we are in the garden, the fight begins, we must go for everyone we see. You will of course use only your swords and dirks, a single shot from an arquebus would set the whole town stirring, and we might be attacked on coming out. Not that with thirteen men such as you I have any misgivings about getting through a little place like that: certainly no one would dare come down to the street; but many of the townsfolk have arquebuses, and they would fire from the windows. In that case, we should have to keep close to the walls of the houses, so much for that. Once you are in the convent garden, you will say in a low voice to every man that shews his face: *Retire;* you will kill with your dirks any that does not immediately obey. I shall go up into the convent by the little door from the garden, with those of you that are near me; three minutes later I shall come down with one or two women whom we shall carry in our arms, without allowing them to walk. We shall then go quickly out of the convent and the town. I shall leave two of you near the gate, they will fire twenty rounds from their arquebuses, one every minute, to frighten the townsfolk and keep them at a distance."

Giulio repeated this explanation a second time.

"Do you quite understand?" he asked his men. "It will

be dark in that hall; on the right the garden, on the left
the courtyard; you must not lose your way."

"Count on us!" cried the soldiers.

Then they went off to drink; the corporal did not follow
them but asked leave to speak to the captain.

"Nothing could be simpler," he said to him, "than your
honour's plan. I have already forced two convents in my
time; this will make the third; but there are not enough
of us. If the enemy oblige us to pull down the wall that
supports the hinges of the second gate, we must bear in
mind that the *bravi* in the barrack will not be idle during
that long operation; they will kill seven or eight of your
men with arquebus shots, and after that they may seize the
lady from us as we come out. That is what happened to
us in a convent near Bologna: they killed five of our men,
we killed eight of theirs, but the captain did not get the
lady. I suggest to your honour two things: I know four
peasants close to this inn where we are now, who have
served gallantly under Sciarra, and for a sequin will fight
all night like lions. They may perhaps steal some silver
from the convent; that does not matter to you, the sin is
upon their heads, you simply pay them to secure a lady,
that is all. My second suggestion is this: Ugone is a
fellow with some education, and very quick; he was a doc-
tor when he killed his brother-in-law and took to the *mac-
chia*. You might send him, an hour before nightfall, to the
gate of the convent; he will ask to take service there, and
will manage so well that he will be admitted to the guard-
room; he will fill the nuns' servants with liquor; more than
that, he is quite capable of wetting the matches of their
arquebuses."

Unfortunately, Giulio accepted the corporal's suggestion.
As the man was leaving his presence, he added:

"We are going to attack a convent, that means *major*

excommunication, and besides, this convent is under the immediate protection of the Madonna. . . ."

"I hear you!" cried Giulio, as though aroused by the last words. "Stay here with me."

The corporal shut the door and came back to repeat the Rosary with Giulio. Their prayers lasted for fully an hour. At dusk, they took the road again.

As midnight struck, Giulio, who had entered Castro by himself about eleven o'clock, returned to fetch his party outside the gate. He entered the town with his eight soldiers, who had been joined by three peasants, well armed; adding to these the five soldiers whom he already had in the town, he found himself at the head of a band of sixteen resolute men; two were disguised as servants, they had put on loose shirts of black cloth to hide their *giacchi* (coats of mail), and they wore no plumes in their caps.

At half past twelve, Giulio, who had cast himself for the part of courier, arrived at a gallop at the gate of the convent, making a great noise, and shouting to the inmates to open at once to a courier sent by the Cardinal. He was pleased to see that the soldiers who answered him through the little window, by the side of the outer gate, were more than half drunk already. Complying with the custom, he handed in his name on a slip of paper; a soldier went to give this to the portress, who had the key of the second gate, and on important occasions had to arouse the Abbess. For three mortal quarters of an hour he was kept waiting for an answer; during this time, Giulio had great difficulty in keeping his troop silent: some of the townsfolk were even beginning timidly to open their windows, when a favourable reply at length arrived from the Abbess. Giulio entered the guard-room by means of a ladder five or six feet in length, which was let down to him from the little window, the *bravi* of the convent not wishing to give themselves the trouble of opening the

great gate: this ladder he climbed, followed by the two
soldiers disguised as servants. As he jumped from the
window sill into the guard-room, he caught the eye of
Ugone; the whole of the guard were drunk, thanks to his
efforts. Giulio told the man in charge that three serv-
ants of the Campireali household, whom he had armed like
soldiers to serve as his escort on the road, had found a
place where there was good brandy for sale, and asked
that they might come up instead of cooling their heels on
the square; this request was unanimously granted. As
for himself, accompanied by his two men, he went down
by the staircase which led from the guard-room into the
passage.

"Try to open the big gate," he said to Ugone.

He himself arrived without the least trouble at the iron
gate. There he found the good portress, who told him
that as it was past midnight, if he entered the convent,
the Abbess would be obliged to report it to the Bishop;
accordingly she sent word asking him to hand his dispatches
to a young sister whom she had sent to receive them. To
which Giulio replied that in the confusion surrounding
the sudden decline of Signor de' Campireali, he had been
given nothing but a simple letter of credit written by the
doctor, and had been ordered to communicate all the de-
tails by word of mouth to the dying man's wife and daugh-
ter, should those ladies still be in the convent, and in any
event to the Lady Abbess. The portress went to convey
this message. There remained by the gate only the young
sister sent down by the Abbess. Giulio while he talked
and joked with her, slipped his hands through the great
iron bars of the gate, and, still laughing, attempted to
open it. The sister, who was very timid, was alarmed
and took the pleasantry amiss; then Giulio, seeing that a
considerable amount of time had passed, was rash enough
to offer her a handful of sequins, begging her to open the

gate for him, adding that he was too tired to wait any
longer. He saw quite well that he was doing a foolish
thing, says the historian: it was with steel and not with
gold that he should have acted, but he had no heart for
that: nothing could have been easier than to seize the
sister, who was not a foot away from him on the other
side of the gate. At his offer of the sequins, the girl took
fright. She said afterwards that, from the way in which
Giulio addressed her, she realised quite clearly that he was
not a mere courier: "He will be the lover of one of our
nuns," she thought, "who has come to keep an assigna-
tion," and she was devout. Seized with horror, she began
to tug with all her strength the rope of a little bell which
hung in the great courtyard, and at once made din enough
to arouse the dead.

"The fight begins," said Giulio to his men; "look out
for yourselves!"

He took his key, and, slipping his arm between the iron
bars, opened the gate, to the complete despair of the young
sister, who fell on her knees and began to recite the *Hail
Mary*, crying out against the sacrilege. Again at this
moment, Giulio ought to have silenced the girl, but had not
the heart to do so: one of his men seized hold of her and
clapped his hand to her mouth.

At that moment Giulio heard an arquebus fired in the
passage behind him. Ugone had opened the main gate; the
remainder of the soldiers were entering without a sound,
when one of the *bravi*, less drunk than the rest, came up to
one of the barred windows, and, in his astonishment at
seeing so many people in the passage, forbade them with
an oath to come any farther. The only thing was to make
no answer and to continue to advance towards the iron
gate; this was what the first of the soldiers did; but the
man who came last of all, and who was one of the peasants
recruited in the afternoon, fired a pistol shot at this servant

who was speaking from the window, and killed him. This
pistol shot, in the dead of night, and the shouts of the
drunken men as they saw their comrade fall, awoke the
soldiers of the convent, who were spending the night in
bed, and had not had an opportunity of tasting Ugone's
wine. Nine or ten of the *bravi* of the convent rushed into
the passage half dressed, and began vigorously to attack
Branciforte's men.

As we have said, this racket began at the moment when
Giulio had succeeded in opening the iron gate. Followed
by his two soldiers, he dashed into the garden, and ran
towards the little door of the boarders' stair; but he was
greeted by five or six pistol shots. His two men fell, he
himself received a bullet in his right arm. These pistol
shots had been fired by Signora de' Campireali's people,
who, by her orders, were spending the night in the garden,
authorised to do so by a special dispensation which she
had obtained from the Bishop. Giulio ran by himself
towards the little door, so well known to him, which led
from the garden to the boarders' stair. He did all he could
to force it open, but it was firmly shut. He searched for
his men, who made no attempt to reply; they were dying;
in the pitch darkness he ran into three of the Campireali
servants against whom he defended himself with his knife.

He ran into the hall, towards the iron gate, to call his
soldiers; he found this gate shut: the pair of heavy iron
rods had been put in position and padlocked by the old
gardeners, who had been aroused by the young sister's
pealing of the bell.

"I am cut off," Giulio said to himself.

He repeated this to his men; in vain did he attempt to
force one of the padlocks with his sword: had he succeeded,
he would have raised one of the iron rods, and opened one
side of the gate. His sword broke in the ring of the pad-
lock; at the same moment he was wounded in the shoulder

by one of the servants who had come in from the garden; he turned round, and resting his back against the iron gate, found himself being attacked by a number of men. He defended himself with his dirk; fortunately, the darkness being unbroken, almost all the sword strokes landed on his coat of mail. He received a painful wound in the knee; he flung himself upon one of the men who had lunged too far to reach him with his sword, killed him by stabbing him in the face with his knife, and was lucky enough to gain possession of the man's sword. From that moment he thought himself safe; he took his stand on the left-hand side of the gate, towards the courtyard. His men, who had hastened to his assistance, fired five or six pistol shots between the iron bars of the gate and sent the servants flying. Nothing was visible in the hall except in the flash of these pistol shots.

"Do not fire in my direction!" cried Giulio to his men.

"Now you are caught like a mouse in a trap," the corporal said to him with the utmost coolness, speaking through the bars; "we have three men killed. We are going to break down the jamb of the gate on the opposite side to where you are; do not come near, the bullets will be falling on us; there seem to be some of the enemy in the garden still."

"Those rascally servants of the Campireali," said Giulio.

He was still speaking to the corporal, when further pistol shots, aimed at the sound of their voices and coming from the part of the hall that led to the garden, were fired at them. Giulio took shelter in the portress's lodge, which was on the left as one entered; to his great joy he found a lamp burning with an almost imperceptible glimmer before the image of the Madonna; he took it with many precautions not to extinguish it; he noticed with regret that he was trembling. He examined the wound in his

knee, which was giving him great pain; the blood was
flowing copiously.

As he cast his eyes round him, he was greatly surprised
at recognising, in a woman who had fainted in a wooden
armchair, little Marietta, Elena's confidential maid; he
shook her vigorously.

"Why, Signor Giulio," she exclaimed, weeping, "are you
going to kill Marietta, your friend?"

"Nothing of the sort; say to Elena that I beg pardon
for having disturbed her sleep, and bid her remember the
Angelus on Monte Cavi. Here is a nosegay which I plucked
in her garden at Albano; but it is stained a little with
blood; wash it before you give it to her."

At that moment, he heard a volley of arquebus shots
fired in the passage; the nuns' *bravi* were attacking his men.

"Tell me, where is the key of the little door?" he said
to Marietta.

"I do not see it; but here are the keys of the padlocks
of the iron bars which keep the great gate shut. You can
get out."

Giulio took the keys and dashed out of the lodge.

"Stop trying to break down the wall," he said to his
soldiers. "I have the key of the gate at last."

There was a moment of complete silence, while he tried
to open a padlock with one of the small keys; he had mis-
taken the key, he tried the other; at length, he opened the
padlock; but just as he was lifting the iron rod, he received
a pistol shot, fired at him almost point blank, in his right
arm. At once he felt that his arm refused to obey him.

"Lift up the iron valet," he cried to his men.

He had no need to tell them.

By the flash of the pistol shot, they had seen the hooked
end of the iron rod almost out of the ring in the gate; when
it was clear of the ring, they let it fall. Then it was pos-

sible to push open one side of the gate; the corporal entered, and said to Giulio, carefully lowering his voice:

"There is nothing more to be done, there are only three or four of us now unwounded, five are dead."

"I am losing blood," replied Giulio. "I feel that I am going to faint; tell them to carry me away."

While Giulio was speaking to the gallant corporal, the soldiers in the guard-room fired three or four more arquebus shots, and the corporal fell dead. Fortunately, Ugone had heard the order given by Giulio, he called two of the soldiers by name, and these picked up their captain. As after all he did not faint, he ordered them to carry him to the end of the garden, to the little door. This order made the men swear; they obeyed, nevertheless.

"A hundred sequins to the man who opens that door!" cried Giulio.

But it resisted the efforts of three furious men. One of the old gardeners, installed in a window on the second floor, fired a number of pistol shots at them, which served to lighten their path.

After vain efforts to break down the door, Giulio fainted completely away; Ugone told the soldiers to carry the captain out as quickly as possible. He himself went into the portress's lodge, out of which he flung little Marietta, telling her in a terrifying voice to make her escape, and never to say that she had recognised him. He pulled out the straw from the bed, broke several chairs and set fire to the room. When he saw the fire well started, he made off as fast as he could run, through a rain of arquebus shots fired by the *bravi* in the convent.

It was not until he had gone some hundred and fifty yards from the Visitation that he found the captain, who, in a dead faint, was being carried rapidly away. A few minutes later, they were out of the town; Ugone called a halt; he had now only four soldiers with him; he sent two

back into the town, with orders to fire their arquebuses
every five minutes.

"Try to find your wounded comrades," he told them, "and
leave the town before daybreak; we are going to follow
the path towards the Croce Rossa. If you can start a fire
anywhere, do so without fail."

When Giulio recovered consciousness, they had gone
three leagues from the town, and the sun was already high
above the horizon. Ugone made his report.

"Your troop consists now of only five men, of whom
three are wounded. Two of the peasants who are alive
have received a reward of two sequins each, and have fled;
I have sent the two men who are not wounded to the
nearest village to fetch a surgeon."

The surgeon, an old man trembling with fear, arrived
presently mounted upon a magnificent ass; the men had
had to threaten to set fire to his house before he would
make up his mind to come. They were obliged also to
dose him with brandy to make him fit to work, so great
was his fear. Finally he set to work; he told Giulio that
his injuries were of no consequence.

"The wound in the knee is not dangerous," he went on,
"but it will make you limp all your life, if you do not keep
absolutely still for the next two or three weeks."

The surgeon dressed the wounds of the men. Ugone
made a sign with his eye to Giulio; two sequins were be-
stowed on the surgeon, who was speechless with gratitude;
then, on the pretext of thanking him, they made him drink
such a quantity of brandy that finally he fell into a deep
sleep. This was what they desired. They carried him
into a neighbouring field, and wrapped four sequins in a
scrap of paper which was slipped into his pocket: it was
the price of his ass, on which were set Giulio and one of
the soldiers who was wounded in the leg. They went to
spend the period of the midday heat in an ancient ruin

by the edge of a pond; they marched all night, avoiding the villages, which were few in number upon that road, and at length, on the third morning, at sunrise, Giulio, carried by his men, awoke in the heart of the forest of la Faggiola, in the charcoal-burner's hut which was his head-quarters.

VI

ON the morning after the fight, the nuns of the Visitation were horrified to find nine dead bodies in their garden and in the passage that led from their outer gate to the gate with the iron bars; eight of their *bravi* were wounded. Never had there been such a panic in the convent; it was true that they had, now and again, heard arquebus shots fired in the square, but never such a quantity of shots fired in the garden, in the middle of the nuns' buildings and beneath their windows. The affair had lasted fully an hour and a half, and during that time the disorder had been complete inside the convent. Had Giulio Branciforte had the least understanding with any of the sisters or boarders, he must have been successful: all that was needed was to open to him one of the many doors that led into the garden; but, wild with indignation and with resentment of what he called the perjury of young Elena, Giulio had sought to carry everything before him by main force. He would have felt that he was failing in his duty to himself, had he confided his plan to anyone who could repeat it to Elena. And yet a single word to her little Marietta would have sufficed to assure his success: she would have opened one of the doors leading into the garden, and one man even appearing in the dormitories of the convent, with that terrible accompaniment of arquebus shots heard from without, would have been obeyed to the letter. At the sound of the first shot, Elena had trembled for the life of her lover, and her one thought had been to fly with him.

How are we to depict her despair when little Marietta

told her of the fearful wound Giulio had received in his
knee, from which she had seen the blood flowing in tor-
rents? Elena detested her own cowardice and pusil-
lanimity:

"I was weak enough to say a word to my mother, and
Giulio's blood has been shed; he might have lost his life
in that sublime assault in which it was his courage that did
everything."

The *bravi,* when admitted to the parlour, had said to the
nuns, who were all agog to hear them, that never in their
lives had they witnessed valour comparable to that of the
young man dressed as a courier who directed the efforts of
the brigands. If all the rest listened to these tales with
the keenest interest, one may judge of the intense passion
with which Elena asked these *bravi* for a detailed account
of the young chief of the brigands. After the long stories
which she made them, and also the old gardeners, tell her,
she felt that she no longer loved her mother at all. There
was indeed a moment of extremely heated discussion be-
tween these two women who had loved each other so ten-
derly on the eve of the fight; Signora de' Campireali was
shocked by the bloodstains which she saw on the flowers
of a certain nosegay from which Elena refused to be parted
for a single instant.

"You ought to throw away those flowers covered with
blood."

"It was I who caused that noble blood to be spilt, and
it flowed because I was weak enough to say a word to you."

"You still love your brother's murderer?"

"I love my husband, who, to my eternal misfortune, was
attacked by my brother."

After this reply, not a single word passed between
Signora de' Campireali and her daughter during the three
more days which the Signora spent in the convent.

On the day following her departure, Elena managed to

escape, taking advantage of the confusion that prevailed
at the two gates of the convent, owing to the presence of a
large number of masons who had been let into the garden
and were engaged in erecting new fortifications there.
Little Marietta and she were disguised as workmen. But
the townsfolk were keeping a strict guard at the gates of
the town. Elena had considerable difficulty in getting out.
Finally, the same small merchant who had conveyed Branci-
forte's letters to her consented to let her pass as his daugh-
ter, and to escort her as far as Albano. There Elena found
a hiding-place with her nurse, whom her generosity had
enabled to open a little shop. No sooner had she arrived,
than she wrote to Branciforte, and the nurse found, not
without great trouble, a man willing to risk his life by
entering the forest of la Faggiola without having the pass-
word of Colonna's troops.

The messenger dispatched by Elena returned after three
days, in great consternation; for one thing, he had been
unable to find Branciforte, and, as the questions which he
continued to put with regard to the young captain had
ended by making him suspected, he had been obliged to
take flight.

"There can be no doubt about it, poor Giulio is dead,"
Elena said to herself, "and it is I that have killed him!
Such was bound to be the consequence of my wretched
weakness and cowardice; he should have loved a strong
woman, the daughter of one of Prince Colonna's captains."

The nurse thought that Elena was going to die. She
went up to the Capuchin convent, standing by the road cut
in the rock, where Fabio and his father had once met the
lovers in the middle of the night. The nurse spoke at
great length to her confessor, and, beneath the seal of the
sacrament, admitted to him that young Elena de' Campi-
reali wished to go and join Giulio Branciforte, her hus-
band, adding that she was prepared to place in the church

of the convent a silver lamp of the value of one hundred
Spanish piastres.

"A hundred piastres!" replied the friar angrily. "And
what will become of our convent, if we incur the anger of
Signor de' Campireali? It was not a hundred piastres,
but a good thousand, that he gave us for going to fetch his
son's body from the battlefield at the Ciampi, not to speak
of the wax."

It must be said to the honour of the convent that two
elderly friars, having discovered where precisely Elena
was, went down to Albano and paid her a visit, originally
with the intention of inducing her by hook or crook to take
up her abode in the palazzo of her family: they knew that
they would be richly rewarded by Signora de' Campireali.
The whole of Albano was ringing with the report of Elena's
flight and of the lavish promises made by her mother to
anyone who could give her news of her daughter. But the
two friars were so touched by the despair of poor Elena,
who believed Giulio Branciforte to be dead, that, so far
from betraying her by revealing to her mother the place in
which she had taken refuge, they agreed to serve as her
escort as far as the fortress of la Petrella. Elena and
Marietta, once more disguised as workmen, repaired on
foot and by night to a certain spring in the forest of la
Faggiola, a league from Albano. The friars had sent mules
there to meet them, and, when day had come, the party set
out for la Petrella. The friars, who were known to be
under the Prince's protection, were greeted everywhere
with respect by the soldiers whom they met in the forest;
but it was not so with the two little men who accompanied
them: the soldiers began by staring at them in the most
forbidding manner and came up to them, then burst out
laughing and congratulated the friars on the charms of
their muleteers.

"Silence, impious wretches; know that all is being done

under Prince Colonna's orders," replied the friars as they proceeded on their way.

But poor Elena was unlucky; the Prince was not at la Petrella, and when, three days later, on his return, he at length granted her an audience, he showed himself most stern.

"Why do you come here, Signorina? What means this ill-advised action? Your woman's chatter has cost the lives of seven of the bravest men in Italy, and that is a thing which no man in his senses will ever forgive you. In this world, one must wish a thing or not wish it. It is doubtless in consequence of similar chatter that Giulio Branciforte has just been declared guilty of sacrilege, and sentenced to be tortured for two hours with red-hot pincers, and then burned as a Jew, he, one of the best Christians I know! How could anyone, without some abominable chattering on your part, have invented so horrible a lie as to say that Giulio Branciforte was at Castro on the day of the attack on the convent? All my men will tell you that they saw him that day here at la Petrella, and that in the evening I sent him to Velletri.

"But is he alive?" Elena cried for the tenth time, bursting into tears.

"He is dead to you," replied the Prince. "You shall never set eyes on him again. I advise you to return to your convent at Castro; try to commit no more indiscretions, and I order you to leave la Petrella within an hour from now. Above all, never mention to anyone that you have seen me, or I shall find a way of punishing you."

Poor Elena was broken-hearted at meeting with such a reception from that famous Prince Colonna, for whom Giulio felt so much respect, and whom she loved because Giulio loved him.

Whatever Prince Colonna might choose to say, this action on Elena's part was by no means ill-advised. If she had come to la Petrella three days earlier, she would have found there Giulio Branciforte; the wound in his knee rendered him incapable of marching, and the Prince had him carried to the market town of Avezzano, in the Kingdom of Naples. At the first news of the terrible sentence upon Giulio Branciforte which, purchased by Signor de' Campireali, denounced him as guilty of sacrilege and of violating a convent, the Prince had seen that, should he have occasion to protect Branciforte, he would have to reckon without three-fourths of his men. This was a sin against the Madonna, to whose protection each of these brigands supposed himself to have a special claim. Had there been a *bargello* in Rome sufficiently daring to come and arrest Giulio Branciforte in the heart of the forest of la Faggiola, he might have been successful.

On reaching Avezzano, Giulio took the name of Fontana, and the men who carried him there were discreet. On their return to la Petrella, they announced with sorrow that Giulio had died on the way, and from that moment each of the Prince's soldiers knew that a dagger would find its way to the heart of any who should pronounce that fatal name.

It was in vain therefore that Elena, on her return to Albano, wrote letter after letter, and spent, on their transmission to Branciforte, all the sequins that she possessed. The two aged friars, who had become her friends, for extreme beauty, says the Florentine chronicler, cannot fail to exercise some sway, even over hearts hardened by the vilest selfishness and hypocrisy; the two friars, we say, warned the poor girl that it was in vain that she might seek to convey a word to Branciforte: Colonna had declared that he was dead, and certainly Giulio would not appear in public again unless the Prince chose. Elena's nurse informed her, with tears, that her mother had at length succeeded in discovering her retreat, and that the

strictest orders had been given that she should be forcibly
taken to the palazzo Campireali, in Albano. Elena realised
that, once inside that palazzo, her imprisonment might be
one of unbounded severity, and that they would succeed in
cutting her off absolutely from any communication with the
outer world, whereas at the Convent of Castro she would
have, for receiving and sending letters, the same facilities
as all the other nuns. Besides, and this was what brought
her to a decision, it was in the garden of that convent that
Giulio had shed his blood for her: she could gaze once more
upon that wooden armchair in the portress's lodge on which
he had sat for a moment to examine the wound in his knee;
it was there that he had given Marietta that nosegay stained
with blood which never left her person. And so she went
sadly back to the Convent of Castro, and here one might
bring her history to an end: it would be well for her, and
for the reader also. For we are now about to observe the
gradual degradation of a noble and generous nature.
Prudent measures and the falsehoods of civilisation, which
for the future are going to assail her on every side, will
take the place of the sincere impulses of vigorous and
natural passions. The Roman chronicler here sets down a
most artless reflexion: because a woman has taken the
trouble to bring into the world a beautiful daughter, she
assumes that she has the talent necessary to direct that
daughter's life, and because, when the daughter is six
years old, she said to her and was justified in saying: "Miss,
put your collar straight," when the daughter is eighteen
and she herself fifty, when the daughter has as much intel-
ligence as her mother and more, the mother, carried away
by the mania for ruling, thinks that she has the right to
direct her daughter's life and even to employ falsehood.
We shall see that it was Vittoria Carafa, Elena's mother,
who, by a succession of adroit measures, most skilfully
planned, brought about the death of that dearly loved

daughter, after keeping her in misery for twelve years, a lamentable result of the mania for ruling.

Before his death, Signor de' Campireali had had the joy of seeing published in Rome the sentence that condemned Giulio Branciforte to be tortured for two hours with red-hot irons in the principal squares of Rome, then to be burned on a slow fire, and his ashes flung into the Tiber. The frescoes in the cloisters of Santa Maria Novella, at Florence, still survive to show us how these cruel sentences upon the sacrilegious were carried out. As a rule, a numerous guard was required to prevent the outraged populace from forestalling the headsmen in their office. Everyone regarded himself as an intimate friend of the Madonna. Signor de' Campireali had had the sentence read over to him again a few moments before his death, and had given the *avvocato* who had procured it his fine estate lying between Albano and the sea. This *avvocato* was by no means devoid of merit. Branciforte was condemned to this terrible punishment, and yet no witness had professed to have recognised him beneath the clothing of that young man disguised as a courier, who seemed to be directing with such authority the movements of the assailants. The magnificence of the reward set all the intriguers of Rome in a stir. There was then at court a certain *fratone* (monk), a deep man and one capable of anything, even of forcing the Pope to give him the Hat; he looked after the affairs of Prince Colonna, and that terrible client earned him great consideration. When Signora de' Campireali saw her daughter once more safely at Castro, she sent for this *fratone*.

"Your Reverence will be lavishly rewarded, if he will be so kind as to help to bring to a successful issue the very simple affair which I am going to explain to him. In a few days' time, the sentence condemning Giulio Branciforte to a terrible punishment is to be published and made

effective in the Kingdom of Naples also. I request Your
Reverence to read this letter from the Viceroy, a relative
of mine, by the way, who deigns to inform me of this news.
In what land can Branciforte seek an asylum? I shall
have fifty thousand piastres conveyed to the Prince, with
the request that he will give the whole sum, or a part of
it, to Giulio Branciforte, on condition that he goes to serve
the King of Spain, my Sovereign, against the rebels in
Flanders. The Viceroy will give a brevet as captain to
Branciforte, and in order that the sentence for sacrilege,
which I hope to have made operative in Spain also, may not
hamper him at all in his career, he will go by the name of
Barone Lizzara; that is a small property which I have in
the Abruzzi, and shall find a way of making over to him,
by means of fictitious sales. I do not suppose Your Rev-
erence has ever seen a mother treat her son's murderér like
this. For five hundred piastres we could long since have
been rid of the hateful creature; but we had no wish to fall
foul of Colonna. Be so good, therefore, as to point out to
him that my respect for his rights is costing me sixty or
eighty thousand piastres. I never wish to hear that Branci-
forte mentioned again; that is all, and you will present my
compliments to the Prince."

The *fratone* said that in two or three days he would be
going in the direction of Ostia, and Signora de' Campireali
handed him a ring worth a thousand piastres.

A few days later, the *fratone* reappeared in Rome, and
told Signora de' Campireali that he had not informed the
Prince of her plan, but that within a month young Branci-
forte would have taken ship for Barcelona, where she would
be able to convey to him, through one of the bankers of
that city, the sum of fifty thousand piastres.

The Prince found considerable difficulty in handling
Giulio. Whatever the risk he must for the future run in
Italy, the young lover could not make up his mind to leave

that country. In vain did the Prince suggest to him that
Signora de' Campireali might die; in vain did he promise
that, in any event, after three years, Giulio might return
to visit his native land; Giulio shed copious tears, but con-
sent he would not. The Prince was obliged to request him
to go, as a personal service to himself; Giulio could refuse
nothing to his father's friend; but, first and foremost, he
wished to take his orders from Elena. The Prince deigned
to take charge of a long letter; and, what was more, gave
Giulio permission to write to her from Flanders once every
month. At length the despairing lover embarked for
Barcelona. All his letters were burned by the Prince, who
did not wish Giulio ever to return to Italy. We have for-
gotten to mention that, although anything like ostentation
was utterly alien to his character, the Prince had felt him-
self obliged to say, in order to bring matters to a successful
issue, that it was he himself who thought fit to assure a
small fortune of fifty thousand piastres to the only son of
one of the most faithful servants of the house of Colonna.

Poor Elena was treated like a Princess in the Convent
of Castro. Her father's death had put her in possession
of a considerable fortune, and a vast inheritance would
accrue to her in time. On the occasion of her father's
death she made a gift of five ells of black cloth to all such
of the inhabitants of Castro or of the district who announced
that they wished to wear mourning for Signor de' Campi-
reali. She was still in the first days of her bereavement
when, by the hand of a complete stranger, a letter was
brought to her from Giulio. It would be hard to describe
the rapture with which that letter was opened, though no
less hard to describe the intense grief which followed her
perusal of it. And yet it was indeed in Giulio's hand-
writing; she examined it with the closest scrutiny. The
letter spoke of love; but what love, great heavens! Never-
theless, it was Signora de' Campireali, who was so clever,

that had composed it. Her intention was to begin the correspondence with seven or eight letters of impassioned love; she wished thus to prepare the way for the next letters, in which the writer's passion would seem to die gradually away.

We may pass briefly over ten years of an unhappy life. Elena supposed herself to be completely forgotten, and yet had scornfully refused the overtures of the most distinguished young noblemen in Rome. She did, however, hesitate for a moment, when mention was made to her of young Ottavio Colonna, the eldest son of the famous Fabrizio, who had received her so coldly, long ago, at la Petrella. She felt that, being absolutely obliged to take a husband in order to provide a protector for the lands which she owned in the Roman States and in the Kingdom of Naples, it would be less repulsive to her to bear the name of a man whom Giulio had once loved. Had she agreed to this marriage, Elena would very soon have found out the truth about Giulio Branciforte. The old Prince Fabrizio spoke often and with enthusiasm of the superhuman valour shown by Colonel Lizzara (Giulio Branciforte), who, just like the heroes of the old romances, was seeking to distract his mind by gallant actions from the unfortunate love affair which made him indifferent to all pleasures. He imagined Elena to be long since married; Signora de' Campireali had surrounded him, too, with falsehood.

Elena was half reconciled to that wiliest of mothers. She, passionately anxious to see her daughter married, asked her friend, old Cardinal Santi Quattro, Protector of the Visitation, who was going to Castro, to announce in confidence to the senior sisters in the convent that his visit to them had been delayed by an act of grace. The good Pope Gregory XIII, moved to pity for the soul of a brigand named Giulio Branciforte, who had once tried to break into their cloister, had been pleased, on learning of his death, to revoke the sentence that declared him guilty of sacrilege, being fully convinced that, beneath the load of such a condemnation, he would never be able to escape from Purgatory, assuming that Branciforte, taken by surprise in Mexico and massacred by rebellious natives, had been so fortunate as to go no farther than Purgatory. This news put the whole Convent of Castro in a stir; it reached the ears of Elena, who at once began to indulge in all the foolish acts of vanity that the possession of a great fortune can inspire in a person who is profoundly vexed. From that moment, she never left her room. It should be explained that, in order to be able to install herself in the little portress's lodge in which Giulio had taken refuge for a moment on the night of the assault, she had had half the convent rebuilt. With infinite pains and, in the sequel, a scandal which it was extremely difficult to hush up, she had succeeded in laying hands on, and in taking into her service the three *bravi* employed by Branciforte who still survived out of the five that had got away from the fight at Castro. Among these was Ugone, now old and crippled by wounds. The arrival of these three men had caused considerable murmuring; but in the end the fear that Elena's proud nature inspired in the whole convent had prevailed, and every day they were to be seen, dressed in her livery, coming to take her orders at the outer grill, and often giving long answers to her questions, which were always on the same subject.

After the six months of seclusion and detachment from all the things of this world which followed the announcement of Giulio's death, the first sensation to awaken this heart already broken by a misfortune without remedy and a long period of boredom was one of vanity.

A little time since, the Abbess had died. According to custom, Cardinal Santi-Quattro, who was still Protector of the Visitation, despite his great age of ninety-two years, had drawn up the list of the three ladies from among whom the Pope would select an Abbess. It required some very serious reason to make His Holiness read the last two names on the list; as a rule he contented himself with running his pen through those names, and the nomination was made.

One day, Elena was at the window of what had been the portress's lodge, and had now become one end of the wing of new buildings erected by her. This window stood not more than two feet above the passage once watered by the blood of Giulio and now forming part of the garden. Elena's eyes were firmly fixed on the ground. The three ladies whose names, as had been known for some days, formed the Cardinal's list of possible successors to the late Abbess, came past Elena's window. She did not see them, and in consequence could not greet them. One of the three ladies was offended, and remarked in a loud voice to the other two:

"A fine thing for a boarder to flaunt her room before everybody."

Aroused by these words, Elena raised her eyes and encountered three hostile stares.

"Very well," she said to herself as she shut the window without greeting them, "I've played the lamb in this convent quite long enough; it's time I became a wolf, if only to give a little variety to the curious gentlemen of the town."

An hour later, one of her servants, dispatched as a courier, carried the following letter to her mother, who for the last ten years had been living in Rome, and had managed to acquire great influence there.

"Most respected Mother,
"Every year you give me three hundred thousand francs upon my birthday; I make use of that money to do foolish

things, perfectly honourable things I must say, but foolish nevertheless. Although it is long since you have mentioned the matter, I know that there are two ways in which I can shew my gratitude for all the thoughtful care you have taken of me. I will never marry, but I would gladly become *Abbess of this Convent;* what has given me the idea is that the three ladies whose names our Cardinal Santi-Quattro has placed on the list which he will present to His Holiness are my enemies, and, whichever of them be chosen, I may expect every sort of annoyance. Offer the usual flowers on my birthday to all the right people; let us first have the nomination postponed for six months, which will make the Prioress of the Convent, my dearest friend, who is now holding the reins, wild with joy. That alone will afford me some happiness, and it is very seldom that I can use that word in speaking of your daughter. I think my idea absurd; but if you see any chance of success, in three days I will take the white veil, eight years of residence in the convent, without a night's absence, entitling me to six months' exemption. The dispensation is never refused, and costs forty scudi.

"I am with respect, my venerable mother," etc.

On reading this letter, Signora de' Campireali's joy knew no bounds. When it reached her, she was bitterly regretting that she had sent word to her daughter of Branciforte's death; she foresaw some mad action, she was even afraid lest her daughter might decide to go to Mexico to visit the spot where Branciforte was said to have been massacred, in which case it was highly probable that she would learn in Madrid the true name of Colonel Lizzara. On the other hand, what her daughter demanded in the letter was the most difficult, one might even say the most preposterous thing in the world. That a young girl who was not even in religion, and was known only for a mad

love affair with a brigand, should be set at the head of a
convent in which all the Roman Princes had relatives pro-
fessed! "But," thought Signora de' Campireali, "they say
that every cause can be pleaded, and, if so, won." In her
reply, Vittoria Carafa gave her daughter grounds for hope;
that daughter, as a rule, wished only for the most absurd
things, but, on the other hand, she very soon tired of them.
In the evening, while seeking any information that, nearly
or remotely, bore upon the Convent of Castro, she learned
that for some months past her friend Cardinal Santi-
Quattro had been extremely cross; he wished to marry his
niece to Don Ottavio Colonna, the eldest son of that Prince
Fabrizio, who has been so often mentioned in the course
of this narrative. The Prince offered him his second son,
Don Lorenzo, because, in order to bolster up his own for-
tune, fantastically compromised by the war which the King
of Naples and the Pope, reconciled at last, were waging
against the brigands of la Faggiola, it was essential that
his eldest son's wife should bring a dowry of six hundred
thousand piastres (3,210,000 francs) to the House of
Colonna. Now Cardinal Santi-Quattro, even by disinherit-
ing in the most preposterous fashion all the rest of his
family, could only offer a fortune of three hundred and
eighty or four hundred thousand piastres.

Vittoria Carafa spent the evening and part of the night
in having these reports confirmed by all the friends of old
Santi-Quattro. Next day, about seven o'clock, she sent in
her name to the old Cardinal.

"Your Eminence," she said to him, "we are neither of us
young; it is useless our trying to deceive one another
by giving fine names to things that are not fine; I have
come to propose to you something mad; all that I can say
in defence of it is that it is not abominable; but I must
admit that I find it supremely ridiculous. When there was
some talk of a marriage between Don Ottavio Colonna and

my daughter Elena, I formed an affection for the young man, and, on the day of his marriage, I will hand over to you two hundred thousand piastres in land or in money, which I shall ask you to convey to him. But, in order to enable a poor widow like myself to make so enormous a sacrifice, I require that my daughter Elena, who is at present twenty-seven years old, and since the age of nineteen has never spent a night out of the convent, be made *Abbess of Castro;* but first of all the election must be postponed for six months; it is all quite canonical."

"What are you saying, Signora?" cried the old Cardinal in horror; "His Holiness himself could not perform what you come here and ask of a poor, helpless old man."

"Did I not tell Your Eminence that the thing was absurd: fools will call it madness; but the people that are well informed of what goes on at court will say that our Excellent Prince, good Pope Gregory XIII, has chosen to reward Your Eminence's long and loyal services by facilitating a marriage which the whole of Rome knows Your Eminence to desire. Besides, it is perfectly possible, quite canonical, I will vouch for it; my daughter is going to take the white veil to-morrow."

"But the simony, Signora!" cried the old man in a terrible voice.

Signora de' Campireali prepared to go.

"What is that paper you are leaving behind you?"

"It is the list of the estates which I should present as the equivalent of two hundred thousand piastres, should that be preferred to ready money; the change of proprietor could be kept secret for a very long time: for instance, the House of Colonna might bring actions against me which I should proceed to lose. . . ."

"But the simony, Signora, the fearful simony!"

"The first thing to be done is to put off the election for

six months; to-morrow I shall call to receive Your Eminence's orders."

I feel that there is need of an explanation, for readers born north of the Alps, of the almost official tone of several passages in this dialogue: let me remind them that, in strictly Catholic countries, the majority of discussions of unpleasant subjects end in the confessional; and then it is anything but a trivial matter whether one has made use of a respectful or of an ironical expression.

In the course of the following day, Vittoria Carafa learned that, owing to a grave error in point of fact which had been discovered in the list of three ladies submitted to fill the vacant post of Abbess of Castro, that election was postponed for six months: the second lady upon the list had a renegade in her family; one of her great-uncles had turned Protestant at Udine.

Signora de' Campireali felt herself impelled to approach Prince Fabrizio Colonna, to whose House she was about to offer so notable an increase in its patrimony. After trying for two days, she succeeded in obtaining an appointment in a village near Rome, but she came away quite alarmed by her audience; she had found the Prince, ordinarily so calm, so greatly taken up with the military glory of Colonel Lizzara (Giulio Branciforte), that she had decided it to be completely useless to ask him to keep silent on that head. The Colonel was to him like a son, and, what was more, a favourite pupil. The Prince spent his time reading and re-reading certain letters that came to him from Flanders. What would become of the cherished plan to which Signora de' Campireali had sacrificed so much in the last ten years, were her daughter to learn of the existence and fame of Colonel Lizzara?

I must pass over in silence a number of circumstances which do, indeed, portray the manners of that age but seem to me wearisome to relate. The author of the Roman manuscript has taken endless pains to arrive at the exact date of these details which I suppress.

Two years after Signora de' Campireali's meeting with Prince Colonna, Elena was Abbess of Castro; but the old Cardinal Santi-Quattro had died of grief after this great act of simony. At that time Castro had as Bishop the handsomest man at the Papal Court, Monsignor Francesco Cittadini, a noble of the city of Milan. This young man, remarkable for his modest graces and his tone of dignity, had frequent dealings with the Abbess of the Visitation, especially with regard to the new cloister with which she proposed to adorn her convent. This young Bishop Cittadini, then twenty-nine years old, fell madly in love with the beautiful Abbess. In the legal proceedings which followed, a year later, a number of nuns, whose evidence was taken, report that the Bishop made his visits to the Convent as frequent as possible, and often said to their Abbess: "Elsewhere I command, and, I am ashamed to say, find some pleasure in doing so; in your presence, I obey like a slave, but with a pleasure that far surpasses that of commanding elsewhere. I find myself under the influence of a superior being; were I to try, I could have no other will than hers, and I would rather see myself, to all eternity, the last of her slaves than reign as king out of her sight."

The witnesses relate that often, in the middle of these elegant speeches, the Abbess would order him to be silent, and in harsh language which implied scorn.

"To tell the truth," another witness goes on, "the Signora used to treat him like a servant; when that happened the poor Bishop would lower his eyes, and begin to weep, but he never went away. He found a fresh excuse every day for coming to the Convent, which greatly scandalised the nuns' confessors and the enemies of the Abbess. But the Lady Abbess was strongly defended by the Prioress, her

dearest friend, who carried on the internal government
under her immediate orders.

"You know, my noble sisters (she used to say), that ever
since that thwarted passion which our Abbess felt in her
earliest girlhood for a soldier of fortune, her ideas have
always been very odd; but you all know that there is this
remarkable element in her character, that she never changes
her mind about people for whom she has shown her con-
tempt. Well, never, in the whole of her life, probably, has
she said so many insulting words as she has uttered in our
presence to poor Monsignor Cittadini. Every day, we see
him submit to treatment which makes us blush for his high
office."

"Yes," replied the scandalised sisters, "but he comes
again the day after; so, after all, he cannot be so ill treated,
and, however that may be, this suggestion of intrigue is
damaging to the reputation of the Holy Order of the
Visitation."

The sternest master would never address to the clumsiest
servant one quarter of the abuse which, day after day, the
proud Abbess heaped upon this young Bishop whose man-
ners were so unctuous; but he was in love, and had brought
from his own country the fundamental maxim that once
an undertaking of this sort has been begun, one has to think
only about the end and not to consider the means.

"After all," said the Bishop to his confidant, Cesare del
Bene, "the true scorn is that felt for the lover who has
desisted from the attack before being compelled to do so
by superior forces."

Now my sad task will be confined to giving an extract,
of necessity extremely dry, from the criminal proceedings
which led to Elena's death. These proceedings, which I
have read in a library the name of which I am obliged to
keep private, occupy no fewer than eight folio volumes.
The questions and arguments are in the Latin tongue, the

answers in Italian. I find that during the month of November, 1572, about eleven o'clock at night, the young Bishop betook himself alone to the door of, the church by which the faithful are admitted throughout the day; the Abbess herself opened this door to him, and allowed him to follow her. She received him in a room which she often occupied, one that communicated by a secret door with the galleries built over the aisles of the church. Barely an hour elapsed before the Bishop, in great bewilderment, was sent packing; the Abbess herself conducted him to the door of the church, and addressed him in these very words:

"Return to your Palace, and leave my sight at once. Farewell, Monsignore; you fill me with horror; I feel that I have given myself to a lackey."

Three months later, however, came Carnival. The people of Castro were famous for the festivities which they held among themselves at this season, the whole town being filled with the clamour of the masquerades. Not one of these failed to pass beneath a little window which gave a feeble light to a certain stable in the Convent. We need not be surprised to hear that three months before Carnival this stable had been converted into a parlour, which was never empty during the days of masquerade. In the midst of all the popular absurdities, the Bishop came past in his coach; the Abbess made him a signal, and, the following night, at one o'clock, he appeared without fail at the door of the church. He entered, but, within three-quarters of an hour, was angrily dismissed. Since the first assignation, in the month of November, he had continued to come to the Convent almost every week. A slight air of rather foolish triumph was to be observed on his face; this everyone noticed, but it had the special effect of greatly shocking the proud nature of the young Abbess. On Easter Monday, among other occasions, she treated him like the meanest of mankind, and addressed to him words which the

humblest workman in the Convent would not have borne.
Nevertheless, a few days later, she gave him a signal, on
receiving which the handsome Bishop presented himself
without fail at the door of the church; she had sent for him
to let him know that she was with child. On hearing this,
says the official account, the young man turned pale with
horror and became absolutely *stupid with fear.* The
Abbess took fever; she sent for the doctor, and made no
mystery to him about her condition. The man knew his
patient's generous nature, and promised to help her out
of the difficulty. He began by putting her in touch with
a woman of humble station, young and good looking, who,
without bearing the title of midwife, had the necessary
acquirements. Her husband was a baker. Elena was
taken with the conversation of this woman, who informed
her that, in order to carry out the plans by which she
hoped to save her, it was necessary that she should have
two other women in her confidence inside the Convent.

"A woman like yourself, well and good, but one of my
equals? Never! Leave my presence."

The midwife withdrew. But, a few hours later, Elena,
feeling it not to be prudent to expose herself to the risk
of the woman's chattering, summoned the doctor, who sent
the woman back to the Convent, where she was liberally
rewarded. This woman swore that, even had she not been
called back, she would never have divulged the secret that
had been confided to her; but she declared once again that,
if there were not, inside the Convent, two women devoted
to the Abbess's interests and conversant with everything,
she herself could have no hand in the matter. (No doubt,
she was thinking of the possible charge of infanticide.)
After prolonged reflexion, the Abbess decided to entrust
this terrible secret to Donna Vittoria, Prioress of the Con-
vent, of the ducal family of C——, and to Donna Bernarda,
daughter of the Marchese P——. She made them swear

on their breviaries that they would never utter a word, even at the stool of penitence, of what she was about to confide to them. The ladies stood frozen with terror. They admit, in their examination, that, having in mind the proud nature of their Abbess, they expected to hear a confession of murder. The Abbess said to them, quite simply and coolly:

"I have failed in all my duties; I am with child."

Donna Vittoria, the Prioress, deeply moved and troubled on account of the ties of friendship which for so many years had bound her to Elena, and not urged by any idle curiosity, exclaimed with tears in her eyes:

"And who is the bold wretch that has committed this crime?"

"I have not told even my confessor; judge whether I am likely to tell you!"

The two ladies at once began to consider the best way of keeping this fatal secret from the rest of the convent. They decided first of all that the Abbess's bed should be removed from her own room, at the very centre of the building, to the Pharmacy, which had just been installed in the most remote part of the Convent, on the third floor of the great wing erected by Elena's generosity. It was in this spot that the Abbess gave birth to a male child. For three weeks the baker's wife had been concealed in the Prioress's apartment. As this woman was hurrying swiftly along the cloister carrying the child, it began to cry, and in her terror she took shelter in the cellar. An hour later, Donna Bernarda, assisted by the doctor, managed to open a little gate in the garden wall; the baker's wife hurriedly left the Convent, and, shortly afterwards, the town. On reaching the open country, still pursued by a wild terror, she took refuge in a little cave to which chance led her among some rocks. The Abbess wrote to Cesare del Bene, the Bishop's confidant and head valet, who hastened to the cave indicated; he was on horseback; he took the infant in his arms, and set off at a gallop for Montefiascone. The child was baptised there in the Church of Saint Margaret, and received the name of Alessandro. The landlady of the local inn had procured a nurse, on whom Cesare bestowed eight scudi: a crowd of women, who had gathered outside the church during the ceremony of baptism, called out persistently to Signor Cesare, demanding the name of the child's father.

"He is a great gentleman of Rome," Cesare told them, "who has allowed himself to make free with a poor village girl like yourselves."

So saying, he vanished.

VII

ALL was going well so far in that immense convent, peopled with more than three hundred inquisitive women; no one had seen anything, no one had heard anything. But the Abbess had given the doctor some handfuls of sequins newly struck from the mint in Rome. The doctor gave several of these pieces to the baker's wife. The woman was pretty and her husband jealous; he searched in her box, found these pieces of gold that shone so brightly, and, supposing them to be the price of her shame, forced her, with a knife at her throat, to tell him from whence they came. After some equivocation, the woman confessed the truth, and peace was made. The couple then began to discuss the use to which they should put so large a sum. The wife wished to pay various debts; but the husband thought it better to buy a mule, which was done. This mule created a scandal among the neighbours, who knew well the poverty of the couple. All the gossips in the town, friend and foe alike, came in turn to ask the baker's wife who was the generous lover who had enabled her to buy a mule. The woman, losing her temper, sometimes replied by telling the truth. One day when Cesare del Bene had been to see the child and came to give an account of his visit to the Abbess, she, although extremely unwell, dragged herself to the grating, and reproached him for the want of discretion shewn by the agents whom he employed. The Bishop, meanwhile, fell ill with fear; he wrote to his brothers in Milan to inform them of the false accusation that was being levelled against him: he appealed to them to come to his rescue. Although seriously ill, he made up his mind to leave Castro; but, before starting, he wrote to the Abbess:

"You know already that all that happened is public property. So, if you have any interest in saving not only my reputation, but perhaps my life, and in order to avoid a greater scandal, you might lay the blame on Gianbattista Doleri, who died two days ago; so that if, in this way, you do not repair your own honour, mine at least shall be no longer imperilled."

The Bishop summoned Don Luigi, Confessor to the Monastery of Castro.

"Deliver this," he said, "into the Lady Abbess's own hands."

She, upon reading this atrocious missive, cried out in the hearing of all that happened to be in the room:

"Thus the foolish virgins deserve to be treated who set the beauty of the body above that of the soul."

The rumour of all that was occurring at Castro came rapidly to the ears of the *terrible* Cardinal Farnese (he had given himself that reputation some years back, because he hoped, at the next conclave, to have the support of the *zealous* Cardinals). He at once gave orders to the *podestà* of Castro to have Bishop Cittadini arrested. All the Bishop's servants, fearing the *question,* took flight. Cesare del Bene alone remained faithful to his master, and swore to him that he would die in torments sooner than reveal anything that might damage him. Cittadini, seeing himself under close guard in his own Palace, wrote again to his brothers, who arrived in haste from Milan. They found him detained in the Ronciglione prison.

I see from the Abbess's first examination that, while admitting her crime, she denied having had relations with the Bishop; her paramour had been Gianbattista Doleri, lawyer to the Convent.

On the 9th of September, 1575, Gregory XIII ordered that the trial should proceed with all haste and with the utmost rigour. A criminal judge, a fiscal and a commissary betook themselves to Castro and Ronciglione. Cesare del Bene, the Bishop's head valet, admitted only that he had taken an infant to a nurse. He was examined in the presence of Donna Vittoria and Donna Bernarda. He was put to the torture on consecutive days; his sufferings were acute; but, true to his word, he admitted only what it was impossible to deny, and the fiscal could extract nothing from him.

When it came to Donna Vittoria and Donna Bernarda, who had witnessed the tortures inflicted on Cesare, they admitted all that they had done. All the nuns were asked the name of the author of the crime; the majority replied that they had heard it said that it was the Bishop. One of the Sister Portresses repeated the offensive words which the Abbess had used to the Bishop when shewing him out of the church. She added: "When people talk in that tone, it means that they have long been making love to one another. And indeed Monsignore, who as a rule was remarkable for his excessive self-assurance, had quite a shamefaced air as he left the church."

One of the sisters, examined in front of the instruments of torture, replied that the author of the crime must be the cat, because the Abbess had it constantly in her arms and was always fondling it. Another sister asserted that the author of the crime must be the wind, because, on days when there was a wind, the Abbess was happy and in a good humour; she would expose herself to the force of the wind on a belvedere which she had had built on purpose; and, when anyone came to ask a favour of her in this spot, she never refused it. The baker's wife, the nurse, the gossips of Montefiascone, frightened by the tortures which they had seen inflicted on Cesare, told the truth.

The young Bishop was ill or feigning illness at Ronciglione, which gave his brothers, supported by the credit and secret influence of Signora de' Campireali, an opportunity of prostrating themselves more than once at the Pope's feet, and asking him that the proceedings might be suspended until the Bishop should have recovered his health. Whereupon the terrible Cardinal Farnese increased the number of the soldiers that were guarding him in his prison. As the Bishop could not be examined, the commissioners began all their sittings by subjecting the Abbess to a fresh examination. One day, after her mother had told her to have courage and to deny everything, she admitted all.

"Why did you first of all inculpate Gianbattista Doleri?"

"Out of pity for the Bishop's cowardice, and, besides, if he succeeds in saving his precious life, he will be able to provide for my son."

After this admission, the Abbess was confined in a room in the Convent of Castro, the walls of which, as well as its vaulting, were eight feet thick; the nuns would never speak of this dungeon without terror, and it went by the name of the monks' room; watch was kept there over the Abbess by three women.

The Bishop's health having slightly improved, three hundred *sbirri* or soldiers came for him to Ronciglione, and he was transported to Rome in a litter; he was confined in the prison called Corte Savella. A few days later, the sisters also were taken to Rome; the Abbess was placed in the Monastery of Santa Marta. Four sisters were inculpated: Donna Vittoria and Donna Bernarda, the sister through whom messages passed, and the portress who had heard the offensive words addressed to the Bishop by the Abbess.

The Bishop was examined by the Auditor of the Chamber, one of the chief personages in the judiciary. Torture was applied once again to the unfortunate Cesare del Bene, who not only admitted nothing, but said things which *caused inconvenience to the public ministry;* these earned him a fresh dose of torture. This preliminary punishment was inflicted similarly upon Donna Vittoria and Donna Bernarda. The Bishop denied everything, with vituperation, but with a fine stubbornness; he gave an account, in the fullest detail, of all that he had done upon the three evenings which he was known to have spent with the Abbess.

Finally the Abbess and Bishop were confronted, and, albeit she continued to tell the truth, she was subjected to torture. As she repeated what she had always said from her first confession, the Bishop, sticking to his part, covered her with abuse.

After a number of other measures, reasonable enough in principle, but marred by that spirit of cruelty which, after the reigns of Charles V and Philip II, prevailed too often in the Italian courts, the Bishop was sentenced to undergo perpetual imprisonment in the Castel Sant' Angelo; the Abbess to be detained for the term of her life in the Convent of Santa Marta, where she was. But already Signora de' Campireali, in the hope of saving her daughter, had set to work to have a subterranean passage burrowed. This passage started from one of those sewers which are relics of the splendour of ancient Rome, and was to end in the deep cellar in which were deposited the mortal remains of the nuns of Santa Marta. This passage, which was barely two feet in width, was walled with planks, to keep back the earth on either side, and was roofed, as it advanced, with pairs of planks arranged like the sides of a capital A.

The tunnel was being bored about thirty feet below ground. The important thing was to carry it in the right direction; at every moment, wells and the foundations of old buildings obliged the workmen to turn aside. Another great difficulty arose as to the disposal of the earth, with which they did not know what to do; it appears that they sprinkled it during the night over all the streets of Rome. The citizens were astonished to see such a quantity of earth, fallen, as one might say, from heaven.

However large the sums Signora de' Campireali might spend in the attempt to save her daughter's life, her subterranean passage would doubtless have been discovered, but Pope Gregory XIII happened to die in 1585, and disorder reigned as soon as the See was vacant.

Elena was far from happy at Santa Marta; one may imagine whether common and distinctly poor nuns shewed zeal in annoying a very rich Abbess convicted of such a crime. She was eagerly awaiting the outcome of her mother's enterprise. But suddenly her heart was caught by strange emotions. Six months had already passed since Fabrizio Colonna, seeing the uncertain state of Gregory XIII's health, and having great plans for the interregnum, had sent one of his officers to Giulio Branciforte, now so widely known in the Spanish armies under the name of Colonel Lizzara. He recalled him to Italy; Giulio was burning to see his native land once more. He landed under a false name at Pescara, a small port on the Adriatic below Chieti, in the Abruzzi, and journeyed over the mountains to la Petrella. The Prince's joy caused general astonishment. He told Giulio that he had sent for him to make him his successor and to give him the command of his troops. To which Branciforte replied that, from the military point of view, it was no longer worth while to continue, as he was easily able to prove; if Spain ever seriously wished to do so, in six months, and at small cost to herself, she could wipe out all the soldiers of fortune in Italy.

"However," young Branciforte added, "if you wish it, Prince, I am ready to take the field. You will always

find in me a successor to the gallant Ranuccio, who was
killed at the Ciampi."

Before Giulio's arrival, the Prince had ordered, as he
alone could order, that no one at la Petrella should dare
to speak of Castro or of the Abbess's trial; the penalty
of death, without hope of respite, was held out as a deter-
rent from any rash word. In the course of the affectionate
greetings with which he welcomed Branciforte, he asked
him on no account to go to Albano without himself, and
his method of carrying out the expedition was to occupy
the town with a thousand of his men, and to post an ad-
vance guard of twelve hundred on the road to Rome. One
may imagine poor Giulio's state when the Prince, having
sent for old Scotti, who was still alive, to the house in
which he had established his headquarters, made him come
up to the room in which he himself was sitting with Branci-
forte. As soon as the two old friends had flung themselves
into each other's arms:

"Now, my poor Colonel," he said to Giulio, "be prepared
for the worst."

Whereupon he snuffed the candle and left the room,
turning the key on the friends.

Next day Giulio, who preferred not to leave his room,
sent to the Prince to ask leave to return to la Petrella,
and not to see him for some days. But his messenger
returned to say that the Prince had disappeared, with all
his troops. During the night, he had heard of the death
of Gregory XIII; he had forgotten his friend Giulio and
was scouring the country. There remained with Giulio
only some thirty men belonging to Ranuccio's old company.
The reader is aware that in those days, during a vacancy
of the See, the law no longer ran, everyone thought of
gratifying his own passions, and there was no force but
brute force; that is why, before the end of the day, Prince
Colonna had already hanged more than fifty of his enemies.

As for Giulio, albeit he had not forty men with him, he made bold to march upon Rome.

All the servants of the Abbess of Castro had remained faithful to her; they were lodged in humble houses near the Convent of Santa Marta. The death agony of Gregory XIII had lasted for more than a week; Signora de' Campireali was eagerly awaiting the troubled days that would follow his death before attacking the final fifty yards of her tunnel. As it had to pass through the cellars of several inhabited houses, she was greatly afraid lest she might be unable to keep from public knowledge the completion of her undertaking.

On the second day after Branciforte's arrival at la Petrella, the three of Giulio's old *bravi,* whom Elena had taken into her service, appeared to have gone mad. Although everyone knew only too well that she was in the strictest isolation, and guarded by nuns who hated her, Ugone, one of the *bravi,* came to the gate of the Convent and made the strangest request that he should be allowed to see his mistress, and without delay. He was refused admission and turned from the door. In his desperation, the man remained outside, and began to distribute *baiocchi* (copper coins) among all the persons employed in the service of the Convent who passed in or out, saying to them these precise words: *"Rejoice with me; Signor Giulio Branciforte has arrived, he is alive: tell this to your friends."*

Ugone's two companions spent the day in bringing him fresh supplies of *baiocchi,* which they continued to distribute day and night, always repeating the same words, until there was not one *baiocco* left. But the three *bravi,* taking turns, continued none the less to keep guard at the gate of the Convent of Santa Marta, still addressing to all that passed them the same words, followed by an obsequious salute: *"Signor Giulio has arrived,"* etc.

These worthy fellows' plan was successful: less than thirty-six hours after the giving of the first *baiocco*, poor Elena, down in her cell, in solitary confinement, knew that *Giulio was alive;* the words threw her into a sort of frenzy: "Oh, my mother!" she cried, "what harm you have wrought me!"

A few hours later, the astonishing news was confirmed by little Marietta, who, by making a sacrifice of all her golden ornaments, obtained leave to accompany the sister who took the prisoner her meals. With tears of joy Elena flung herself into her arms.

"This is very pleasant," she said to her, "but I shall not be with you much longer."

"Indeed no!" said Marietta. "I am sure that before this Conclave is ended, your imprisonment will be changed to an ordinary banishment."

"Ah, my dear, to see Giulio again! And to see him, with this guilt on my head!"

In the middle of the third night after this conversation, part of the floor of the church fell in with a loud noise; the nuns of Santa Marta thought that their convent was going to collapse. Their commotion was extreme, everyone was calling out that there had been an earthquake. About an hour after the subsidence of the marble pavement of the church, Signora de' Campireali, preceded by the three *bravi* in Elena's service, made her way into the dungeon by the underground passage.

"Victory, victory, Signora!" cried the *bravi*.

Elena was in a mortal fear; she thought that Giulio Branciforte was with them. She was quite reassured, and her features resumed their stern expression when the men told her that they were escorting Signora de' Campireali, and that Giulio was still at Albano, which he had just invaded with several thousand troops.

She waited for some moments, and then Signora de'

Campireali appeared; she was walking with great difficulty, on the arm of her *scudiere,* who was in full costume, with sword on hip; but his gorgeous coat was all soiled with earth.

"Oh, my dear Elena, I have come to rescue you!" cried Signora de' Campireali.

"And how do you know that I wish to be rescued?"

Signora de' Campireali was left speechless; she stared helplessly at her daughter; she seemed greatly agitated.

"Well, my dear Elena," she said at length, "fate compels me to confess to you an action which was perhaps natural enough, after the misfortunes that had befallen our family, but of which I repent, and beg that you will forgive me for it: Giulio . . . Branciforte . . . is alive . . ."

"And it is because he is alive that I have no wish to live."

Signora de' Campireali did not at first grasp her daughter's meaning, then she besought her with the most tender supplications; but she could obtain no answer. Elena had turned to her crucifix and was praying without listening to her. In vain, for a whole hour, did Signora de' Campireali make every effort to win from her a word or a look. At length, her daughter, losing patience, said to her:

"It was beneath the marble of this crucifix that his letters were hidden, in my little room at Albano; it had been better to let my father stab me! Go, and leave some gold with me."

As Signora de' Campireali tried to continue speaking to her daughter, disregarding the signs of alarm shewn by her *scudiere,* Elena lost patience.

"Let me, at least, have an hour of freedom; you have poisoned my life, you wish to poison my death as well."

"We shall still have command of the passage for two or three hours; I venture to hope that you will change your mind!" exclaimed Signora de' Campireali, bursting into tears.

And she made her way out by the underground passage.

"Ugone, stay with me," said Elena to one of her *bravi*, "and see you are well armed, my lad, for you may have to defend me. Let me see your dirk, your sword, your dagger."

The old soldier shewed her these weapons, all in good condition.

"Good; now wait there, outside my cell; I am going to write Giulio a long letter which you will hand to him yourself; I do not wish it to pass through any hands but yours, having nothing with which to seal it. You may read the whole of the letter. Put in your pockets all the gold my mother has left there, I need for myself only fifty sequins; place them on my bed."

Having said these words, Elena sat down to write.

"I have not the least doubt of you, my dear Giulio; if I take my departure, it is because I should die of grief in your arms, at the sight of what would have been my happiness, had I not committed a sin. You are not to imagine that I have ever loved any creature in the world after you; far from it, my heart was filled with the bitterest contempt for the man whom I admitted to my room. My sin was solely one of distraction, and, if you like, of wantonness. Think that my spirit, greatly weakened after the futile attempt which I made at la Petrella, where the Prince whom I revered, because you loved him, received me so cruelly; think, I say, that my spirit, greatly weakened, had been assailed by twelve years of falsehood. Everything round me was lying and false, and I knew it. I received first of all some thirty letters from you; imagine the rapture with which, at first, I used to tear them open. But, as I read them, my heart froze. I examined the

writing, I recognised your hand, but not your heart. Think
that this first falsehood cankered the essence of my life, so
that I could open a letter in your writing without any
pleasure! The detestable announcement of your death
finally killed in me anything that might yet survive from
the happy days of our youth. My first intention, as you
can well understand, was to go to see with my eyes and
touch with my hands the Mexican shore upon which they
said that the savages had massacred you; had I carried
out that idea . . . we should be happy now, for, in Madrid,
whatever the number and craftiness of the spies that a
watchful hand might have managed to dispose round about
me, as I myself would have appealed to every heart in
which there remained a trace of pity and of goodness, it
is probable that I should have arrived at the truth; for
already, my Giulio, your gallant deeds had attracted the
attention of the whole world towards you, and perhaps
someone in Madrid knew that you were Branciforte.
Would you like me to tell you what prevented our happi-
ness? First of all, the memory of the atrocious, humiliating
reception the Prince gave me at la Petrella; what a chain
of obstacles to surmount between Castro and Mexico! You
see, my heart had already lost its motive power. Then I
had an impulse of vanity. I had erected huge buildings
in the Convent, in order to be able to take as my own room
the portress's lodge, in which you took shelter on the night
of the assault. One day, I was looking at the ground
which, for my sake, you had watered with your blood; I
heard a contemptuous utterance, raised my head, saw spite-
ful faces; to avenge myself, I decided to become Abbess.
My mother, who knew quite well that you were alive, made
heroic efforts to secure that preposterous nomination. The
position was nothing, for me, but a source of trouble; it
completed the debasement of my nature; I took pleasure
often in proving my power by the suffering of others; I

committed acts of injustice. I saw myself, at the age of thirty, virtuous according to the world, rich, respected, and yet completely wretched. Then there appeared that poor man, who was goodness itself, but foolishness personified. The effect of his foolishness was that I bore with his first suggestions. My heart had been made so wretched by everything that surrounded me after your departure, that it had no longer the strength to resist the slightest temptation. Shall I confess to you something really indelicate? Yes, for I remember that everything is permitted to the dead. When you read these lines, the worms will be devouring this so-called beauty, which should have been all yours. Well, I must out with this matter which distresses me; I did not see why I should not make trial of the coarser side of love, like all our Roman ladies; I had a lascivious thought, but I was never able to give myself to that man without a feeling of horror and disgust which destroyed all the pleasure. I saw you always at my side, in the garden of our palazzo at Albano, when the Madonna inspired in you that thought, apparently so noble, but one that has, after my mother, been the bane of our lives. You were not at all threatening, but tender and good as you always were, you looked at me, then I felt moments of anger with that other man, and went so far as to beat him with all my strength. This is the whole truth, my dear Giulio: I did not wish to die without telling you it, and I thought also that perhaps this conversation with you might take away from me the idea of dying. It makes me see all the more clearly what would have been my joy on greeting you again, had I kept myself worthy of you. I order you to live and to continue that military career which caused me so much joy when I heard of your success. What would my joy have been, great God, had I received your letters, especially after the battle of Achenne! Live, and recall often to your mind the memory of Ranuccio, killed at the

Ciampi, and that of Elena, who, not to read a reproach in your eyes, lies dead at Santa Marta."

Having written this, Elena went up to the old soldier, whom she found sleeping; she took his dirk from him, without his noticing the loss, then aroused him.

"I have finished," she told him; "I am afraid of our enemies' seizing the passage. Go at once, take my letter which is on the table, and give it yourself to Giulio, *yourself,* do you understand? In addition to that, give him this handkerchief, tell him that I love him no more at this moment than I have always loved him, *always,* remember!"

Ugone was on his feet but made no move.

"Off with you!"

"Signora, have you really decided? Signor Giulio loves you so!"

"And I too, I love him, take the letter and give it to him yourself."

"Very well, may God bless you as you deserve!"

Ugone went and speedily returned; he found Elena dead; the dirk was in her heart.

VANINA VANINI

VANINA VANINI

or

SOME PARTICULARS OF
THE LATEST ASSEMBLY OF CARBONARI
DISCOVERED IN THE STATES
OF THE CHURCH

IT was a spring evening in 182—. All Rome was astir: the Duca di B——, the famous banker, was giving a ball in his new palazzo on the Piazza di Venezia. All the most sumptuous treasures that the arts of Italy, the luxury of Paris and London can furnish had been collected for the adornment of this palace. The gathering was immense. The fair, retiring beauties of noble England had intrigued for the honour of being present at this ball; they arrived in crowds. The most beautiful women of Rome vied with them for the prize of beauty. A girl whom her sparkling eyes and ebon tresses proclaimed of Roman birth entered, escorted by her father; every eye followed her. A singular pride was displayed in her every gesture.

One could see the foreigners who entered the room struck by the magnificence of this ball. "None of the courts of Europe," they were saying, "can compare with this."

Kings have not a palace of Roman architecture: they are obliged to invite the great ladies of their courts; the Duca di B—— invites only lovely women. This evening he had been fortunate in his invitations; the men seemed dazzled. Amid so many remarkable women it was hard to decide which was the most beautiful: the award was for some time undetermined; but at length Principessa Vanina Vanini, the girl with the raven hair and fiery eye, was proclaimed queen of the ball. Immediately the foreigners and the young Romans, deserting all the other rooms, crowded into the room in which she was.

Her father, Principe Don Asdrubale Vanini, had wished her to dance first of all with two or three Sovereign Princes from Germany. She then accepted the invitations of certain extremely handsome and extremely noble Englishmen; their starched manner irritated her. She appeared to find more pleasure in teasing young Livio Savelli, who seemed deeply in love. He was the most brilliant young man in Rome, and a Prince to boot; but, if you had given him a novel to read, he would have flung the book away after twenty pages, saying that it made his head ache. This was a disadvantage in Vanina's eyes.

Towards midnight a report ran through the ball-room, which caused quite a stir. A young carbonaro, in detention in the Castel Sant' Angelo, had escaped that evening, with the help of a disguise, and, with an excess of romantic daring, on coming to the outermost guard-room of the prison, had attacked the soldiers there with a dagger; but he had been wounded himself, the *sbirri* were pursuing him through the streets, following the track of his blood, and hoped to recapture him.

While this story was going round, Don Livio Savelli, dazzled by the charms and the success of Vanina, with whom he had just been dancing, said to her as he led her back to her seat, being almost mad with love:

"Why, in heaven's name, what sort of person could please you?"

"This young carbonaro who has just made his escape,"

was Vanina's reply; "he at least has done something more than take the trouble to be born."

Principe Don Asdrubale approached his daughter. He is a wealthy man who for the last twenty years has kept no accounts with his steward, who lends him his own income at a high rate of interest. If you should pass him in the street, you would take him for an elderly actor; you would not notice that his fingers were loaded with five or six enormous rings set with huge diamonds. His two sons became Jesuits, and afterwards died insane. He has forgotten them, but it vexes him that his only daughter, Vanina, declines to marry. She is already nineteen, and has refused the most brilliant suitors. What is her reason? The same that led Sulla to abdicate, her *contempt for the Romans.*

On the day after the ball, Vanina remarked that her father, the most casual of men, who never in his life had taken the trouble to carry a key, was very careful in shutting the door of a little stair which led to an apartment on the third floor of the palazzo. The windows of this apartment looked on to a terrace planted with orange trees. Vanina went out to pay some calls in Rome; on her return, the main door of the palazzo was blocked with the preparations for an illumination, the carriage drove in through the courtyards at the back. Vanina raised her eyes, and saw with astonishment that one of the windows of the apartment which her father had so carefully closed was now open. She got rid of her companion, climbed up to the attics of the palazzo and after a long search succeeded in finding a small barred window which overlooked the orange tree terrace. The open window which she had observed from below was within a few feet of her. Evidently the room was occupied; but by whom? Next day, Vanina managed to secure the key of a small door which opened on to the terrace planted with orange trees.

She stole on tiptoe to the window, which was still open. It was screened by a sunblind. Inside the room was a bed, and somebody in the bed. Her first impulse was to retire; but she caught sight of a woman's gown flung over a chair. On looking more closely at the person in the bed, she saw that this person was fair, and evidently quite young. She had no longer any doubt that it was a woman. The gown flung over the chair was stained with blood; there was blood also on the woman's shoes placed beneath a table. The stranger moved in the bed; Vanina saw that she had been wounded. A great bandage stained with blood covered her bosom; this bandage was fastened with ribbons only; it was not a surgeon's hand that had so arranged it. Vanina noticed that èvery day, about four o'clock, her father shut himself up in his own rooms, and then went to visit the stranger; presently he came downstairs and took his carriage to call upon the Contessa Vitelleschi. As soon as he had left the house, Vanina went up to the little terrace, from which she could see the stranger. Her compassion was strongly aroused towards this young woman who was in such a plight; she tried to imagine what could have befallen her. The bloodstained gown that lay on the chair appeared to have been stabbed with a dagger. Vanina could count the rents in it. One day she saw the stranger more distinctly: her blue eyes were fastened on the ceiling; she seemed to be praying. Presently tears welled in those lovely eyes; the young Princess could hardly refrain from addressing her. Next day, Vanina ventured to hide on the little terrace before her father came upstairs. She saw Don Asdrubale enter the stranger's room; he was carrying a small basket in which were provisions. The Prince appeared ill at ease, and said but little. He spoke so low that, although the window stood open, Vanina could not overhear his words. He soon left.

"That poor woman must have very terrible enemies," Vanina said to herself, "for my father, who is so careless by nature, not to dare to confide in anyone and to take the trouble to climb a hundred and twenty steps every day."

One evening, as Vanina was cautiously extending her head towards the stranger's window, their eyes met, and she was discovered. Vanina fell on her knees, crying: "I love you, I am your devoted servant."

The stranger beckoned to her to come in.

"How can I apologise to you?" cried Vanina; 'how offensive my foolish curiosity must appear to you! I swear to keep your secret, and, if you insist on it, I will never come again."

"Who would not be delighted to see you?" said the stranger. "Do you live in this palazzo?"

"Certainly," replied Vanina. "But I see that you do not know me: I am Vanina, Don Asdrubale's daughter."

The stranger looked at her with an air of surprise, then went on:

"Please let me hope that you will come to see me every day; but I should prefer the Prince not to know of your visits."

Vanina's heart beat violently; the stranger's manner seemed to her most distinguished. This poor young woman had doubtless given offence to some powerful man; possibly in a moment of jealousy she had killed her lover. Vanina could not conceive any common reason for her trouble. The stranger told her that she had received a wound in the shoulder, which had penetrated her breast and gave her great pain. Often she found her mouth filled with blood.

"And you have no surgeon!" cried Vanina.

"You know that in Rome," said the stranger, "the surgeons have to furnish the police with an exact report of all the injuries that they treat. The Prince is kind enough to dress my wounds himself with the bandage you see here."

The stranger refrained with the most perfect taste from any commiseration of her accident; Vanina loved her madly. One incident, however, greatly surprised the young Princess, which was that in the middle of a conversation which was certainly most serious the stranger had great difficulty in suppressing a sudden impulse to laughter.

"I should be happy," Vanina said to her, "to know your name."

"I am called Clementina."

"Very well, dear Clementina, to-morrow at five I shall come to see you."

Next day Vanina found her new friend in great pain.

"I am going to bring you a surgeon," said Vanina as she embraced her.

"I would rather die," said the stranger. "Would you have me compromise my benefactors?"

"The surgeon of Monsignor Savelli-Catanzara, the Governor of Rome, is the son of one of our servants," Vanina answered firmly; "he is devoted to us, and in his position has no fear of anyone. My father does not do justice to his loyalty; I am going to send for him."

"I do not want any surgeon!" cried the stranger with a vivacity which surprised Vanina. "Come and see me, and if God is to call me to Himself, I shall die happy in your arms."

On the following day the stranger was worse.

"If you love me," said Vanina as she left her, "you will see a surgeon."

"If he comes, my happiness is at an end."

"I am going to send to fetch him," replied Vanina.

Without saying a word, the stranger seized hold of her, and took her hand, which she covered with kisses. A long

silence followed; tears filled the stranger's eyes. At
length she let go Vanina's hand, and with the air of one
going to her death, said to her:

"I have a confession to make to you. The day before
yesterday, I lied when I said that my name was Clemen-
tina; I am an unhappy carbonaro . . ."

Vanina in her astonishment thrust back her chair, and
presently rose.

"I feel," went on the carbonaro, "that this confession
is going to make me forfeit the one blessing which keeps
me alive; but I should be unworthy of myself were I to
deceive you. My name is Pietro Missirilli; I am nineteen;
my father is a poor surgeon at Sant' Angelo in Vado, I
myself am a carbonaro. Our *venuta* was surprised; I was
brought, in chains, from the Romagna to Rome. Cast
into a dungeon lighted day and night by a lamp, I lay
there for thirteen months. A charitable soul conceived
the idea of helping me to escape. I was dressed as a
woman. As I was leaving the prison and passing by the
guard at the outer gate, one of them cursed the carbonari;
I dealt him a blow. I swear to you that it was not a piece
of vain bravado, but simply that I was not thinking. Pur-
sued by night through the streets of Rome after that act of
folly, stabbed with bayonet wounds, I had begun to lose
my strength, I entered a house the door of which stood
open, I heard the soldiers coming in after me, I sprang
into a garden; I fell to the ground within a few feet of
a woman who was walking there."

"Contessa Vitelleschi! My father's mistress," said
Vanina.

"What! Has she told you?" cried Missirilli. "How-
ever that may be, this lady, whose name must never be
uttered, saved my life. As the soldiers were coming into
her house to seize me, your father took me away in his
carriage. I feel very ill: for some days this bayonet wound

in my shoulder has prevented me from breathing. I am going to die, and in despair, since I shall not see you again."

Vanina had listened with impatience; she swiftly withdrew from the room. Missirilli read no pity in those lovely eyes, but only the signs of a proud nature which had been deeply offended.

When it was dark, a surgeon appeared; he was alone. Missirilli was in despair; he was afraid that he would never see Vanina again. He questioned the surgeon, who bled him and made no reply. A similar silence on each of the days that followed. Pietro's eyes never left the window on the terrace by which Vanina used to enter; he was very miserable. Once, about midnight, he thought he could see someone in the dark on the terrace: was it Vanina?

Vanina came each night to press her face against the panes of the young carbonaro's window.

"If I speak to him," she said to herself, "I am lost! No, I must never see him again!"

Having come to this resolution, she recalled, in spite of herself, the affection that she had formed for this young man when she had so stupidly taken him for a woman. After so pleasant an intimacy, must she then forget him? In her most reasonable moments, Vanina was alarmed by the change that was occurring in her ideas. Ever since Missirilli had told her his name, all the things of which she was in the habit of thinking were, so to speak, wrapped in a veil of mist, and appeared to her now only at a distance.

A week had not gone by before Vanina, pale and trembling, entered the young carbonaro's room with the surgeon. She had come to tell him that he must make the Prince promise to let his place be taken by a servant. She was not in the room for ten seconds; but some days later she came back again with the surgeon, from a sense of humanity. One evening, although Missirilli was much better, and Vanina had no longer the excuse of being alarmed for his life, she ventured to come unaccompanied. On seeing her, Missirilli was raised to a pinnacle of joy, but he was careful to conceal his love; whatever happened, he was determined not to forget the dignity befitting a man. Vanina, who had come into the room blushing a deep crimson, and dreading amorous speeches, was disconcerted by the noble and devoted, but by no means tender friendliness with which he greeted her. She left without his making any attempt to detain her.

A few days later, when she returned, the same conduct, the same assurances of respectful devotion and eternal gratitude. So far from being occupied in putting a check on the transports of the young carbonaro, Vanina asked herself whether she alone were in love. This girl, hitherto so proud, was bitterly aware of the full extent of her folly. She made a pretence of gaiety, and even of coldness, came less frequently, but could not bring herself to abandon her visits to the young invalid.

Missirilli, burning with love, but mindful of his humble birth and of what he owed to himself, had made a vow that he would not stoop to talk of love unless Vanina were to spend a week without seeing him. The pride of the young Princess contested every inch of ground.

"After all," she said to herself at length, "if I see him, it is for my own sake, to please myself, and I will never confess to him the interest that he arouses in me."

She paid long visits to Missirilli, who talked to her as he might have done had there been a score of persons present. One evening, after she had spent the day hating him, and promising herself that she would be even colder and more severe with him than usual, she told him that she loved him. Soon there was nothing left that she could withhold from him.

Great as her folly may have been, it must be admitted that Vanina was sublimely happy. Missirilli no longer thought of what he believed to be due to his dignity as a man; he loved as people love for the first time at nineteen and in Italy. He felt all the scruples of "impassioned love," going so far as to confess to this haughty young Princess the stratagem which he had employed to make her love him. He was astounded by the fulness of his happiness. Four months passed rapidly enough. One day the surgeon set his patient at liberty. "What am I to do now?" thought Missirilli; "lie concealed in the house of one of the most beautiful people in Rome? And the vile tyrants who kept me for thirteen months in prison without ever allowing me to see the light of day will think they have disheartened me! Italy, thou art indeed unfortunate, if thy sons forsake thee for so slight a cause!"

Vanina never doubted that Pietro's greatest happiness lay in remaining permanently attached to herself; he seemed only too happy; but a saying of General Bonaparte echoed harshly in the young man's heart and influenced the whole of his conduct with regard to women. In 1796, as General Bonaparte was leaving Brescia, the municipal councillors who were escorting him to the gate of the city told him that the Brescians loved freedom more than any of the Italians.

"Yes," he replied, "they love to talk about it to their mistresses."

Missirilli said to Vanina with a visible air of constraint: "As soon as it is dark, I must go out."

"Be careful to come in again before daybreak; I shall be waiting for you."

"By daybreak I shall be many miles from Rome."

"Very well," said Vanina coldly, "and where are you going?"

"To the Romagna, to have my revenge."

"As I am rich," Vanina went on with perfect calmness, "I hope that you will let me supply you with arms and money."

Missirilli looked at her for some moments without moving a muscle; then, flinging himself into her arms:

"Soul of my life," he said to her, "you make me forget everything, even my duty. But the nobler your heart is, the better you must understand me."

Vanina wept freely, and it was agreed that he should not leave Rome until the following night.

"Pietro," she said to him on the morrow, "you have often told me that a well-known man, a Roman Prince, for instance, with plenty of money at his disposal, would be in a position to render the utmost services to the cause of freedom, should Austria ever be engaged abroad, in some great war."

"Undoubtedly," said Pietro in surprise.

"Very well, you have a stout heart; all you lack is an exalted position: I have come to offer you my hand and an income of two hundred thousand lire. I undertake to obtain my father's consent."

Pietro fell at her feet; Vanina was radiant with joy.

"I love you passionately," he told her; "but I am a humble servant of the Fatherland; the more unhappy Italy is, the more loyal I should be to her. To obtain Don Asdrubale's consent, I shall have to play a sorry part for many years. Vanina, I decline your offer."

Missirilli made haste to bind himself by this utterance. His courage was failing him.

"My misfortune," he cried, "is that I love you more than life itself, that to leave Rome is for me the most agonising torture. Oh, that Italy were set free from the barbarians! With what joy would I set sail with you to go and live in America."

Vanina's heart was frozen. The refusal of her hand

had dealt a blow to her pride; but presently she threw herself into Missirilli's arms.

"Never have you seemed so adorable," she cried; "yes, my little country surgeon, I am yours for ever. You are a great man, like our ancient Romans."

All thoughts of the future, every depressing suggestion of common sense vanished; it was a moment of perfect love. When they were able to talk reasonably:

"I shall be in the Romagna almost as soon as you," said Vanina. "I am going to have myself sent to the baths of la Porretta. I shall stop at the villa we have at San Niccolò, close to Forlì. . . ."

"There I shall spend my life with you!" cried Missirilli.

"My lot henceforward is to dare all," Vanina continued with a sigh. "I shall ruin myself for you, but no matter. . . . Will you be able to love a girl who has lost her honour?"

"Are you not my wife," said Missirilli, "and the object of my lifelong adoration? I shall know how to love and protect you."

Vanina was obliged to go out, on social errands. She had barely left Missirilli before he began to feel that his conduct was barbarous.

"What is the *Fatherland?*" he asked himself. "It is not a person to whom we owe gratitude for benefits received, or who may suffer and call down curses on us if we fail him. The *Fatherland* and *Freedom* are like my cloak, a thing which is useful to me, which I must purchase, it is true, when I have not acquired it by inheritance from my father; but after all I love the Fatherland and Freedom because they are both useful to me. If I have no use for them, if they are to me like a cloak in the month of August, what is the good of purchasing them, and at an enormous price? Vanina is so beautiful! She has so singular a nature! Others will seek to attract her; she will forget me. What

woman is there who has never had more than one lover?
Those Roman Princes, whom I despise as citizens, have
so many advantages over me! They must indeed be at-
tractive! Ah, if I go, she will forget me, and I shall lose
her for ever."

In the middle of the night, Vanina came to see him; he
told her of the uncertainty in which he had been plunged,
and the criticism to which, because he loved her, he had
subjected that great word "Fatherland." Vanina was very
happy.

"If he were absolutely forced to choose between his
country and me," she told herself, "I should have the
preference."

The clock of the neighbouring church struck three, the
time had come for a final leave-taking. Pietro tore him-
self from the arms of his mistress. He had begun to de-
scend the little stair, when Vanina, restraining her tears,
said to him with a smile:

"If you had been nursed by some poor woman in the
country, would you do nothing to shew your gratitude?
Would you not seek to repay her? The future is uncertain,
you are going on a journey through the midst of your
enemies: give me three days out of gratitude, as if I were
a poor woman, and to pay me for the care I have taken
of you."

Missirilli stayed. At length he left Rome. Thanks to
a passport bought from a foreign embassy, he returned in
safety to his family. This was a great joy to them; they
had given him up for dead. His friends wished to cele-
brate his home-coming by killing a carabiniere or two
(such is the title borne by the police in the Papal States).

"We must not, when it is not necessary, kill an Italian
who knows how to handle arms," said Missirilli; "our
country is not an island, like happy England: it is soldiers

that we need to resist the intervention of the Sovereigns of Europe."

Some time later Missirilli, hard pressed by the carabinieri, killed a couple of them with the pistols which Vanina had given him. A price was set on his head.

Vanina did not appear in the Romagna: Missirilli imagined himself forgotten. His vanity was hurt; his thoughts began to dwell upon the difference in rank which divided him from his mistress. In a moment of weakness and regret for his past happiness it occurred to him that he might return to Rome to see what Vanina was doing. This mad idea was beginning to prevail over what he believed to be his duty when one evening the bell of a church in the mountains sounded the Angelus in a singular fashion, and as though the ringer were thinking of something else. It was the signal for the assembling of the *venuta* of carbonari which Missirilli had joined on his arrival in Romagna. That night, they all met at a certain hermitage in the woods. The two hermits, drugged with opium, knew nothing of the use to which their little dwelling was being put. Missirilli, who arrived in great depression, learned there that the leader of the *venuta* had been arrested, and that he, a young man not twenty years old, was about to be elected leader of a *venuta* which included men of fifty and more, who had taken part in all the conspiracies since Murat's expedition in 1815. On receiving this unexpected honour, Pietro felt his heart beat violently. As soon as he was alone, he determined to give no more thought to the young Roman who had forgotten him, and to devote his whole mind to the duty of *freeing Italy from the barbarians.*[1]

Two days later, Missirilli saw in the reports of arrivals

[1] *Liberar l'Italia de' barbari*: the words used by Petrarch in 1350, and since then repeated by Julius II, Machiavelli and Conte Alfieri.

and departures which were supplied to him, as leader of
the *venuta,* that the Principessa Vanina had just arrived
at her villa of San Niccolò. The sight of that name caused
him more uneasiness than pleasure. It was in vain that
he imagined himself to be proving his loyalty to his country
by undertaking not to fly that very evening to the villa of
San Niccolò; the thought of Vanina, whom he was neg-
lecting, prevented him from carrying out his duty in a
reasonable manner. He saw her next day; she loved him
still as in Rome. Her father, who wished her to marry,
had delayed her departure. She brought him two thousand
sequins. This unexpected assistance served admirably to
accredit Missirilli in his new office. They had daggers
made for them in Corfu; they won over the Legate's private
secretary, whose duty it was to pursue the carbonari. Thus
they obtained a list of the clergy who were acting as spies
for the government.

It was at this time that the organisation was completed
of one of the least senseless conspiracies that have been
planned in unhappy Italy. I shall not enter here into
irrelevant details. I shall merely say that if success had
crowned the attempt, Missirilli would have been able to
claim a good share of the glory. At a signal from him,
several thousands of insurgents would have risen, and
awaited, armed, the coming of their superior leaders. The
decisive moment was approaching when, as invariably
happens, the conspiracy was paralyzed by the arrest of
the leaders.

Immediately on her arrival in Romagna, Vanina felt that
his love of his country would make her young lover forget
all other love. The young Roman's pride was stung. She
tried in vain to reason with herself; a black melancholy
seized her: she found herself cursing freedom. One day
when she had come to Forlì to see Missirilli, she was power-

less to check her grief, which until then her pride had managed to control.

"Truly," she said to him, "you love me like a husband; that is not what I have a right to expect."

Soon her tears flowed; but they were tears of shame at having so far lowered herself as to reproach him. Missirilli responded to these tears like a man preoccupied with other things. Suddenly it occurred to Vanina to leave him and return to Rome. She found a cruel joy in punishing herself for the weakness that had made her speak. After a brief interval of silence, her mind was made up; she would feel herself unworthy of Missirilli if she did not leave him. She rejoiced in the thought of his pained surprise when he should look around for her in vain. Presently the reflexion that she had not succeeded in obtaining the love of the man for whom she had done so many foolish things moved her profoundly. Then she broke the silence, and did everything in the world to wring from him a word of love. He said, with a distracted air, certain quite tender things to her; but it was in a very different tone that, in speaking of his political enterprises, he sorrowfully exclaimed:

"Ah, if this attempt does not succeed, if the government discovers it again, I give up the struggle."

Vanina remained motionless. For the last hour, she had felt that she would never look upon her lover again. The words he had now uttered struck a fatal spark in her mind. She said to herself:

"The carbonari have had several thousands from me. No one can doubt my devotion to the conspiracy."

Vanina emerged from her musings only to say to Pietro:

"Will you come and spend the night with me at San Niccolò? Your meeting this evening can do without you. To-morrow morning, at San Niccolò, we can take the air together; that will calm your agitation and restore the cool judgment you require on great occasions."

Pietro agreed.

Vanina left him to make ready for the journey, locking the door, as usual, of the little room in which she had hidden him.

She hastened to the house of one of her former maids who had left her service to marry and keep a small shop in Forlì. On reaching the house, she wrote in haste on the margin of a Book of Hours which she found in the woman's room, an exact indication of the spot at which the *venuta* of carbonari was to assemble that evening. She concluded her denunciation with the words: "This *venuta* is composed of nineteen members; their names and addresses are as follows." Having written this list, which was quite accurate except that the name of Missirilli was omitted, she said to the woman, on whom she could rely:

"Take this book to the Cardinal Legate; make him read what is written in it, and give you back the book. Here are ten sequins; if the Legate ever utters your name, your death is certain; but you will save my life if you make the Legate read the page I have just written."

All went well. The Legate's fear prevented him from standing upon his dignity. He allowed the humble woman who asked to speak with him to appear before him with only a mask, but on condition that her hands were tied. In this state the shop-keeper was brought into the presence of the great personage, whom she found entrenched behind an immense table, covered with a green cloth.

The Legate read the page in the Book of Hours, holding it at a distance, for fear of some subtle poison. He gave it back to the woman, and did not have her followed. In less than forty minutes after she had left her lover, Vanina, who had seen her former maid return, appeared once more before Missirilli, imagining that for the future he was entirely hers. She told him that there was an extraordinary commotion in the town; patrols of carabinieri were to be seen in streets along which they never went as a rule.

"If you will take my advice," she went on, "we will start this very instant for San Niccolò."

Missirilli agreed. They proceeded on foot to the young Princess's carriage, which, with her companion, a discreet and well-rewarded confidant, was waiting for her half a league from the town.

Having reached the San Niccolò villa, Vanina, disturbed by the thought of what she had done, multiplied her attentions to her lover. But when speaking to him of love she felt that she was playing a part. The day before, when she betrayed him, she had forgotten remorse. As she clasped her lover in her arms, she said to herself:

"There is a certain word which someone may say to him, and once that word is uttered, then and for all time, he will regard me with horror."

In the middle of the night, one of Vanina's servants came boldly into her room. This man was a carbonaro, and she had never known it. So Missirilli had secrets from her, even in these matters of detail. She shuddered. The man had come to inform Missirilli that during the night, at Forlì, the houses of nineteen carbonari had been surrounded and they themselves arrested as they were returning from the *venuta*. Although taken unawares, nine of them had escaped. The carabinieri had managed to convey ten to the prison of the citadel. On their way in, one of these had flung himself down the well, which was deep, and had killed himself.

Vanina lost countenance; happily Pietro did not observe her; he could have read her crime in her eyes. . . . "At the present moment," the servant went on, "the Forlì garrison is lining all the streets. Each soldier is close enough to the next to be able to speak to him. The inhabitants

cannot cross from one side of the street to the other except
at the places where there is an officer posted."

After the man had left them, Pietro remained pensive for
a moment only.

"There is nothing to be done for the present," he said
finally.

Vanina was half dead; she trembled under her lover's
gaze.

"Why, what is the matter with you?" he asked her.

Then his thoughts turned to other things, and he ceased
to look at her. Towards midday she ventured to say to
him:

"And so another *venuta* has been surprised; I hope that
you are going to be undisturbed now for some time."

"Quite undisturbed," replied Missirilli with a smile
which made her shudder.

She went to pay a necessary call upon the parish priest
of San Niccolò, who might perhaps be a spy of the Jesuits.
On returning to dine at seven o'clock, she found the little
room in which her lover had been concealed empty. Beside
herself with alarm, she ran over the whole house in search
of him. In despair, she returned to the little room, and it
was only then that she saw a note; she read:

"I am going to give myself up to the Legate; I despair
of our cause; heaven is against us. Who has betrayed us?
Evidently the wretch who flung himself down the well.
Since my life is of no use to poor Italy, I do not wish that
my comrades, seeing that I alone have not been arrested,
should imagine that I have sold them. Farewell; if you
love me, try to avenge me. Destroy, crush the scoundrel
who has betrayed us, even if he should be my own father."

Vanina sank down on a chair, half unconscious, and
plunged in the most agonizing grief. She could not utter
a word; her eyes were parched and burning.

At length she flung herself upon her knees:

"Great God!" she cried, "hear my vow; yes, I will punish the scoundrel who has betrayed them; but first I must set Pietro free."

An hour later, she was on her way to Rome. Her father had long been pressing her to return. During her absence, he had arranged her marriage with Principe Livio Savelli. Immediately on Vanina's arrival, he spoke to her of this marriage, in fear and trembling. Greatly to his surprise, she consented from the first. That evening, at Contessa Vitelleschi's, her father presented to her, semi-officially, Don Livio; she conversed with him freely. He was the most exquisite young man, and had the finest horses of any; but although he was admitted to have plenty of intelligence, he was regarded as so frivolous that he was held in no suspicion by the government. Vanina reflected that, by first of all turning his head, she might make a useful agent of him. As he was the nephew of Monsignor Savelli-Catanzara, Governor of Rome and Minister of Police, she supposed that the government spies would not dare to follow him.

After shewing herself most kind, for some days, to the charming Don Livio, Vanina broke to him that he could never be her husband; he had, according to her, too light a mind.

"If you were not a mere boy," she told him, "your uncle's clerks would have no secrets for you. For instance, what action is being taken with regard to the carbonari who were surprised the other day at Forlì?"

Don Livio came to inform her, a few days later, that all the carbonari taken at Forlì had escaped. She let her large black eyes rest on him with a bitter smile of the most profound contempt, and did not condescend to speak to him throughout the evening. Two days later, Don Livio came to confess to her, blushing as he did so, that he had been misinformed at first.

"But," he told her, "I have secured a key to my uncle's room; I see from the papers I found there that a *congregation* (or commission) composed of the Cardinals and prelates who are most highly considered is meeting in the strictest secrecy, and discussing whether it would be better to try these carbonari at Ravenna or in Rome. The nine carbonari taken at Forlì and their leader, a certain Missirilli, who was fool enough to give himself up, are at this moment confined in the castle of San Leo.[1]

At the word "fool," Vanina gripped the Prince with all her strength.

"I wish," she said, "to see the official papers myself, and to go with you into your uncle's room; you must have misread what you saw."

At these words, Don Livio shuddered; Vanina asked a thing that was almost impossible; but the girl's eccentric nature intensified his love for her. A few days later, Vanina, disguised as a man and wearing a neat little jacket in the livery of the casa Savelli, was able to spend half an hour among the most secret documents of the Minister of Police. She started with joyful excitement when she came upon the daily report on *Pietro Missirilli, on remand.* Her hands shook as she seized the paper. On reading the name again, she felt as though she must faint. As they left the palace of the Governor of Rome, Vanina permitted Don Livio to embrace her.

"You are coming very well," she told him, "through the tests to which I mean to subject you."

After such a compliment, the young Prince would have set fire to the Vatican to please Vanina. That evening, there was a ball at the French Ambassador's; she danced

---

[1] Near Rimini in Romagna. It was in this castle that the famous Cagliostro died; the local report is that he was smothered there.

frequently, and almost always with him. Don Livio was wild with joy; he must be kept from thinking.

"My father sometimes acts oddly," Vanina said to him one day; "this morning he dismissed two of his servants, who came to me in tears. One asked me to find him a place with your uncle the Governor of Rome; the other, who served as a gunner under the French, wishes to be employed in the Castel Sant' Angelo."

"I will take them both into my service," said the young Prince impulsively.

"Is that what I am asking you to do?" Vanina answered haughtily. "I repeat to you word for word the request made by these poor men; they must obtain what they have asked for, and nothing else."

It was the hardest thing imaginable. Monsignor Catanzara was the most serious of men, and admitted into his household only people well known to himself. In the midst of a life filled, apparently, with every pleasure, Vanina, crushed by remorse, was most unhappy. The slow course of events was killing her. Her father's man of business had supplied her with money. Ought she to fly from the paternal roof and make her way to the Romagna to try to compass her lover's escape? Absurd as this idea was, she was on the point of putting it into execution, when chance took pity on her.

Don Livio said to her:

"The ten carbonari of the Missirilli *venuta* are going to be transferred to Rome, except that they will be executed in the Romagna after they have been sentenced. My uncle obtained the Pope's authority for that this evening. You and I are the only two people in Rome who know this secret. Are you satisfied?"

"You are growing into a man," replied Vanina; "you may make me a present of your portrait."

On the day before that on which Missirilli was to reach

Rome, Vanina found an excuse for going to Città Castellana. It is in the prison of this town that carbonari are lodged on their way from the Romagna to Rome. She saw Missirilli in the morning, as he was leaving the prison: he was chained by himself upon a cart; he struck her as very pale but not at all despondent. An old woman tossed him a bunch of violets; Missirilli thanked her with a smile.

Vanina had seen her lover, her mind seemed to revive; she felt fresh courage. Long before this she had procured a fine advancement for the Abate Cari, Chaplain of the Castel Sant' Angelo, in which her lover was to be confined; she had chosen this worthy priest as her confessor. It is no small matter in Rome to be the confessor of a Princess, who is the Governor's niece.

The trial of the carbonari from Forlì did not take long. To be revenged for their transfer to Rome, which it had been unable to prevent, the "ultra" party had the commission which was to try them packed with the most ambitious prelates. Over this commission presided the Minister of Police.

The law against the carbonari is clear: the men from Forlì could entertain no hope; they fought for their lives nevertheless by every possible subterfuge. Not only did their judges condemn them to death, but several were in favour of cruel tortures, amputation of the right hand, and so forth. The Minister of Police, whose fortune was made (for one leaves that office only to assume the Hat), was in no need of amputated hands: on submitting the sentence to the Pope, he had the penalty commuted to some years of imprisonment for all the prisoners. The sole exception was Pietro Missirilli. The Minister regarded the young man as a dangerous fanatic, in addition to which he had already been sentenced to death as guilty of the murder of the two carabinieri whom we have mentioned. Vanina knew of the sentence and its commutation within a few minutes of the Minister's return from seeing the Pope.

On the following evening, when Monsignor Catanzara returned to his palace about midnight, his valet was not to be found; the Minister, somewhat surprised, rang several times; finally an aged and half-witted servant appeared; the Minister, losing patience, decided to undress himself. He turned the key in his door; it was a hot night: he took off his coat, and flung it in a heap upon a chair. This coat, thrown with excessive force, went beyond the chair, and fell against the muslin curtain of the window, behind which it outlined the figure of a man. The Minister sprang swiftly to his bedside and seized a pistol. As he was returning to the window, a man quite young, wearing his livery, came towards him, pistol in hand. Seeing him advance, the Minister raised his own pistol to his eye; and was about to fire. The young man said to him with a laugh:

"Why, Monsignor, do not you recognise Vanina Vanini?"

"What is the meaning of this ill-timed foolery?" replied the Minister angrily.

"Let us discuss the matter calmly," said the girl. "In the first place, your pistol is not loaded."

The Minister, taken aback, found that this was so; whereupon he took out a dagger from the pocket of his waistcoat.[1]

---

[1] A Roman prelate would doubtless be incapable of commanding an Army Corps with gallantry, as happened more than once in the case of a divisional general who was Minister of Police in Paris, at the time of the Malet conspiracy; but he would never allow himself to be held up so simply as this in his own house. He would be too much afraid of the satirical comment of his colleagues. A Roman who knows himself to be hated always goes about well armed. It has not been thought necessary to give authority for various other slight differences between Parisian and Roman habits of speech and behaviour. So

Vanina said to him with a charming little air of authority:
"Let us be seated, Monsignore."

And she took her seat calmly upon a sofa.

"Are you alone, tell me that?" said the Minister.

"Absolutely alone, I swear to you!" cried Vanina.

The Minister took care to verify this assurance: he made a tour of the room and searched everywhere; after which he sat down upon a chair three paces away from Vanina.

"What object could I have," said Vanina with a calm and winning air, "in attempting the life of a man of moderate views, who would probably be succeeded by some weak hothead, capable of destroying himself and other people?"

"What is your purpose then, Signorina?" said the Minister crossly. "This scene is highly improper and must not continue."

"What I am going to add," Vanina went on haughtily, suddenly forgetting her gracious manner, "concerns you rather than myself. The life of the carbonaro Missirilli must be saved: if he is executed, you shall not outlive him by a week. I have no interest in the matter; the foolish action of which you complain was planned, first of all, for my own amusement, and also to oblige one of my friends. I wished," went on Vanina, resuming her air of good breeding, "to do a service to a man of talent, who will shortly become my uncle, and ought, one would say, to enhance considerably the fame and fortune of his house."

The Minister ceased to appear angry: Vanina's beauty no doubt contributed to this rapid alteration. Monsignor Catanzara's fondness for pretty women was well known in Rome, and in her disguise as a footman of the casa Savelli, with close-fitting silk stockings, a red waistcoat, her little

far from minimising these differences, we have felt it our duty to indicate them boldly. The Romans whom we are describing have not the honour to be French.

sky-blue jacket with its silver braid, and the pistol in her hand, Vanina was irresistible.

"My future niece," said the Minister, almost laughing, "you are doing a very foolish thing, and it will not be the last."

"I trust that so wise a person as yourself," replied Vanina, "will keep my secret, especially from Don Livio; and to bind you, my dear uncle, if you grant me the life of my friend's favourite, I will give you a kiss."

It was by continuing the conversation in this half jocular tone, with which Roman ladies know how to discuss the most serious matters, that Vanina succeeded in giving to this interview, begun pistol in hand, the semblance of a visit paid by the young Principessa Savelli to her uncle the Governor of Rome.

Soon Monsignor Catanzara, while rejecting with lofty scorn the idea that he could let himself be influenced by fear, found himself explaining to his niece all the difficulties that he would meet in trying to save Missirilli's life. As he talked, the Minister strolled up and down the room with Vanina; he took a decanter of lemonade that stood on the mantelpiece and poured some of the liquid into a crystal glass. Just as he was about to raise it to his lips, Vanina took it from him, and, after holding it in her hand for some time, let it fall into the garden, as though by accident. A moment later the Minister took a chocolate drop from a comfit box. Vanina seized it from him, saying with a smile:

"Take care, now; everything in the room is poisoned; for your death was intended. It was I who obtained a reprieve for my future uncle, that I might not enter the house of Cavelli absolutely empty handed."

Monsignor Catanzara, greatly astonished, thanked his niece, and gave her good reason to hope for the life of Missirilli.

"Our bargain is made!" cried Vanina, "and in proof of it, here is your reward," she said, kissing him.

The Minister accepted his reward.

"You must understand, my dear Vanina," he went on, "that I myself do not like bloodshed. Besides, I am still young, though to you perhaps I may appear very old, and I may survive to a time in which blood spilt to-day will leave a stain."

Two o'clock was striking when Monsignor Catanzara accompanied Vanina to the little gate of his garden.

A couple of days later, when the Minister appeared before the Pope, considerably embarrassed by the action which he had to take, His Holiness began:

"First of all, I have a favour to ask of you. There is one of those carbonari from Forlì who is under sentence of death; the thought of him keeps me awake at night: the man's life must be spared."

The Minister, seeing that the Pope had made up his mind, raised a number of objections, and ended by writing out a decree or *motu proprio,* which the Pope signed, regardless of precedent.

Vanina had thought that she might perhaps obtain her lover's reprieve, but that an attempt would be made to poison him. The day before, Missirilli had received from the Abate Cari, his confessor, several little packets of ship's biscuit, with a warning not to touch the food supplied by the State.

Having afterwards learned that the carbonari from Forlì were to be transferred to the Castle of San Leo, she decided to attempt to see Missirilli as he passed through Città Castellana; she arrived in that town twenty-four hours ahead of the prisoners; there she found the Abate Cari, who had preceded her by several days. He had obtained the concession from the gaoler that Missirilli might hear mass, at midnight, in the prison chapel. This was not all: if Missirilli would consent to have his arms and legs chained together, the gaoler would withdraw to the door of the chapel, in such a way as not to lose sight of the prisoner, for whom he was responsible, but to be out of hearing of anything he might say.

The day which was to decide Vanina's fate dawned at last. As soon as morning came, she shut herself up in the prison chapel. Who could describe the thoughts that disturbed her mind during that long day? Did Missirilli love her sufficiently to forgive her? She had denounced his *venuta*, but she had saved his life. When reason prevailed in her tormented brain, Vanina hoped that he would consent to leave Italy with her: if she had sinned, it was from excess of love. As four was striking, she heard in the distance, on the cobbled street, the hooves of the carabinieri's horses. The sound of each hoof-beat seemed to strike an echo from her heart. Presently she could make out the rumbling of the carts in which the prisoners were being conveyed. They stopped in the little piazza outside the prison; she saw two carabinieri lift up Missirilli, who was alone on one cart, and so loaded with irons that he could not move. "At least he is alive," she said to herself, the tears welling into her eyes, "they have not poisoned him yet." The evening was agonising; the altar lamp, hanging at a great height, and sparingly supplied with oil by the gaoler, was the only light in the dark chapel. Vanina's eyes strayed over the tombs of various great nobles of the middle ages who had died in the adjoining prison. Their statues wore an air of ferocity.

All sounds had long ceased; Vanina was absorbed in her sombre thoughts. Shortly after midnight had struck, she thought she heard a faint sound, like the fluttering of a bat. She tried to walk, and fell half fainting against the altar rail. At that moment, two spectres appeared close beside her, whom she had not heard come in. They were the gaoler and Missirilli, so loaded with chains as to be almost smothered in them. The gaoler opened a dark lantern which he placed on the altar rail, by Vanina's side, in such a way as to give him a clear view of his prisoner. He then withdrew to the other end of the chapel, by the door. No sooner had the gaoler moved away than Vanina flung herself on Missirilli's bosom. As she clasped him in her arms, she felt only the cold edges of his chains. "To whom does he owe these chains?" was her thought. She felt no pleasure in embracing her lover. This grief was followed by another even more poignant; she fancied for a moment that Missirilli was aware of her crime, so frigid was his greeting.

"Dear friend," he said to her at length, "I regret the affection that you have formed for me; I seek in vain to discover what merit in me has been capable of inspiring it. Let us return, believe me, to more Christian sentiments, let us forget the illusions which hitherto have been leading us astray; I cannot belong to you. The constant misfortune that has dogged my undertakings is due perhaps to the state of mortal sin into which I have so often fallen. To listen only to the counsels of human prudence, why was not I arrested with my friends, on that fatal night at Forlì? Why, in the moment of danger, was I not found at my post? Why has my absence then furnished grounds for the most cruel suspicions? I had another passion besides that for the liberation of Italy."

Vanina could not get over her surprise at the change in Missirilli. Without being perceptibly thinner, he had the air of a man of thirty. Vanina attributed this change to the ill treatment which he had undergone in prison, and burst into tears.

"Ah!" she said, "the gaolers promised so faithfully that they would treat you well."

The fact was that at the approach of death all the religious principles consistent with his passion for the liberation of Italy had revived in the heart of the young carbonaro. Gradually Vanina realised that the astonishing change which she had remarked in her lover was entirely moral, and in no way the effect of bodily ill treatment. Her grief, which she had supposed to have reached its extreme limit, was intensified still further.

Missirilli was silent; Vanina seemed to be on the point of being suffocated by her sobs. He spoke, and himself also appeared slightly moved:

"If I loved any single thing in the world, it would be you, Vanina; but, thanks be to God, I have now but one object in life; I shall die either in prison or in seeking to give Italy freedom."

Another silence followed; evidently Vanina was incapable of speech: she attempted to speak, but in vain. Missirilli went on:

"Duty is cruel, my friend; but if it were not a little difficult to perform, where would be the heroism? Give me your word that you will not attempt to see me again."

So far as the chain that was wound tightly about him would allow, he made a slight movement with his wrist and held out his fingers to Vanina.

"If you will accept the advice of one who was once dear to you, be sensible and marry the deserving man whom your father has chosen for you. Do not confide in him anything that may lead to trouble; but, on the other hand, never seek to see me again; let us henceforward be strangers to one another. You have advanced a considerable sum for the service of the Fatherland; if ever it is delivered from its tyrants, that sum will be faithfully repaid to you in national bonds."

Vanina was crushed. While he was speaking, Pietro's eye had gleamed only at the moment when he mentioned the Fatherland.

At length pride came to the rescue of the young Princess;
she had brought with her a supply of diamonds and small
files. Without answering Missirilli, she offered him these.

"I accept from a sense of duty," he told her, "for I must
seek to escape; but I will never see you, I swear it by
this latest token of your bounty. Farewell, Vanina; promise
me never to write, never to attempt to see me; leave me
wholly to the Fatherland, I am dead to you: farewell."

"No," replied Vanina, grown furious, "I wish you to
know what I have done, led on by the love that I bear you."

She then related to him all her activities from the moment
when Missirilli had left the villa of San Niccolò to give
himself up to the Legate. When her tale was finished:

"All this is nothing," said Vanina: "I have done more,
in my love for you."

She then told him of her betrayal.

"Ah, monster," cried Pietro, mad with rage, hurling him-
self upon her; and sought to crush her to the ground with
his chains.

He would have succeeded but for the gaoler, who came
running at the sound of her cries. He seized Missirilli.

"There, monster, I will not owe anything to you," said
Missirilli to Vanina, flinging at her, as violently as his
chains would allow him, the files and diamonds, and he
moved rapidly away.

Vanina was left speechless. She returned to Rome: and
the newspapers announce that she has just been married
to Principe Don Livio Savelli.

THE END

New Directions Paperbooks—A Partial Listing

For complete listing request free catalog from
New Directions, 80 Eighth Avenue, New York 10011   †Bilingual